Better Homes and Gardens®

Christmas from the Heart

Home for the Holidays

BETTER HOMES AND GARDENS® BOOKS
Des Moines, Iowa

BETTER HOMES AND GARDENS® BOOKS
An Imprint of Meredith® Books

CHRISTMAS FROM THE HEART
Vice President and Editorial Director: Elizabeth P. Rice
Editor-in-Chief: Carol Field Dahlstrom
Managing Editor: Susan Banker
Art Director: Gayle Schadendorf
Copy Chief: Eve Mahr
Senior Writer: Barbara Hickey
Senior Graphic Designer: Bridget Sandquist
Technical Editor: Colleen Johnson
Administrative Assistant: Peggy Daugherty
Contributing Technical Illustrator: Chris Neubauer
Contributing Technical Editor: Barbara Barton Smith
Production Manager: Douglas Johnston

President, Book Group: Joseph J. Ward
Vice President, Retail Marketing: Jamie L. Martin
Vice President, Direct Marketing: Timothy Jarrell
Publisher, Craftways: Maureen Ruth

Meredith Corporation
Chairman of the Executive Committee: E.T. Meredith III
Chairman of the Board and Chief Executive Officer: Jack D. Rehm
President and Chief Operating Officer: William T. Kerr

All of us at Better Homes and Gardens® Books are dedicated to providing you with the information and ideas you need to create beautiful and useful projects. We guarantee your satisfaction with this book for as long as you own it. We welcome your questions, comments, or suggestions. Please write to us at: Cross Stitch & Country Crafts®, Better Homes and Gardens® Books, RW 235, 1716 Locust Street, Des Moines, IA 50309-3023.

If you would like to order additional copies of any of our books, call 1-800-678-2803 or check with your local bookstore.

Cover: Photograph by Hopkins Associates

Our "Mark of Excellence" craft seal assures you that every project in this publication has been constructed and checked under the direction of the crafts experts at Better Homes and Gardens® Cross Stitch & Country Crafts® magazine.

Our seal assures you that every recipe in *Christmas from the Heart* has been tested in the Better Homes and Gardens® Test Kitchen. This means that each recipe is practical and reliable, and meets our high standards of taste appeal.

There is magic in the air at Christmastime—
a special kind of love that comes from the heart and
radiates to all who celebrate the season. We hear it in the
sweet Christmas carols that warm the frosty winter nights.
We smell it when we enter holiday homes filled with the
warm fragrances of holiday baking. We see it when our
houses and neighborhoods are all aglow with twinkling
colorful lights and our homes are adorned with the handmade treasures we've created. And we feel it when our
children throw their arms around us and giggle for no other
reason than the contagious excitement of the season. We
hope that this book will delight you with glorious
holiday visions, excite you with creative and
festive ideas, and inspire you to create just
the kind of Christmas we all love
and remember, a

Christmas
from the Heart

Contents

I'll Be Home for Christmas

Make your loved ones' holiday homecoming picture perfect with this remarkable collection of festive foods and crafts.

Deck the Halls

Fill your home with the spirit of the season by crafting the heartwarming projects shown on these pages.

Have Yourself a Merry Little Christmas

Create our clever quick-and-easy projects and still have time to share the season's joy with family and friends.

Hark, the Herald Angels Sing

These glorious angels to paint, stitch, sew, and bake are heavenly treasures for your home or to give as gifts.

O Christmas Tree

Decorated and interpreted in a variety of ways, our Christmas trees present a delightful array of crafting ideas.

Silent Night, Holy Night

The true meaning of Christmas comes alive with the help of this lovely collection of costumes, crafts, and food.

Santa Claus Is Comin' to Town

The twinkle in Santa's eye is necessary for a jolly holiday, so we've gathered a charming group for you to bake, stitch, and sew.

Here We Come A-Wassailing

Here you'll find festive fare to share with guests and creatively packaged treats for the celebrations of the holiday season.

I'll Be Home for Christmas

You'll be home for Christmas and the warmth of the holiday season will glow with our abundant collection of festive food and crafts created especially for you and your family. We've used a glorious palette of colors chosen from natural fruit motifs as the inspiration for many of the ideas in this chapter, creating an elegant and picture-perfect holiday homecoming.

Merry Christmas and welcome home!

PHOTOGRAPHER: HOPKINS ASSOCIATES

Holiday Bounty Vest

*Begin your celebration at home
wearing our elegant fruit-motif
cross-stitched vest. The vest is stitched on
Heatherfield fabric with front panels
displaying a cornucopia of beautiful fruits.
The vest back is designed with a full
wreath of fruits and ribbons. Stitch the
colorful motifs first and then sew into a
vest using a purchased pattern.
Charts begin on page 18 and
instructions are on page 20.*

DESIGNER: LINDA GORDANIER JARY
PHOTOGRAPHER: HOPKINS ASSOCIATES

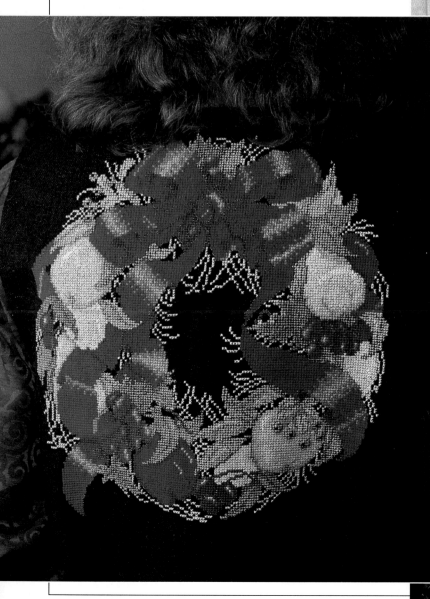

8

Fruit and Magnolia Fan

Apples, magnolias, and the traditional symbol of hospitality—the pineapple—are combined to make our colonial-looking mantel or door piece. The magnolia leaves fan around the other fruits forming a semicircle of colorful bounty. Instructions are on page 21.

Peaches and Grapes Floorcloth

Painted on natural canvas, our stylized-fruit floorcloth will surely welcome the family home. The fruit pattern is painted in the center of the canvas with highlights added for a traditional look. An ivy border surrounds the fruit motifs and is accented with neutral stripes that appear to frame this exquisite piece. Instructions begin on page 22; full-size patterns are on pages 24–25.

DESIGNERS: FAN, GERRY BAUMAN; FLOORCLOTH, SUSAN CORNELISON
PHOTOGRAPHER: HOPKINS ASSOCIATES

Mirror Place Cards

Our quick-to-make place cards are constructed from metallic doilies, tiny mirrors, and colorful jewels. Each glittering place card is personalized by writing the guest's name with a paint pen. Instructions are on page 27.

Poinsettia Appliqué Sweater

Poinsettias of crimson suede fabric, appliquéd on a purchased powder pink sweater, set the stage for a lovely homecoming. Each poinsettia is embellished with a golden bead center for added sparkle. Full-size patterns and instructions begin on page 28.

DESIGNER: MARGARET SINDELAR ● PHOTOGRAPHER: HOPKINS ASSOCIATES

Creamy Caramel-Pecan Rolls and Puffy Name Bread

Greet Christmas morning with easy, but luscious, holiday breads. Our Creamy Caramel-Pecan Rolls are made from frozen dough. They can be shaped the day before and refrigerated overnight for just-baked perfection.

Make personalized Puffy Name Bread up to two months in advance and store in the freezer until the big day. Recipes are on pages 29 and 31.

PHOTOGRAPHER: HOPKINS ASSOCIATES

14

Serendipity Wreath

Welcome the holiday season with a colorful wreath. This one features a potpourri of exotic dried fruits and fragrant spices. Hang it in the traditional manner to greet guests at the door, arrange it on the piano as shown below, or add candles to create the glowing centerpiece on page 9. It will share warm yule cheer throughout the Christmas season. Instructions are on page 31.

DESIGNER: GERRY BAUMAN ● PHOTOGRAPHER: HOPKINS ASSOCIATES

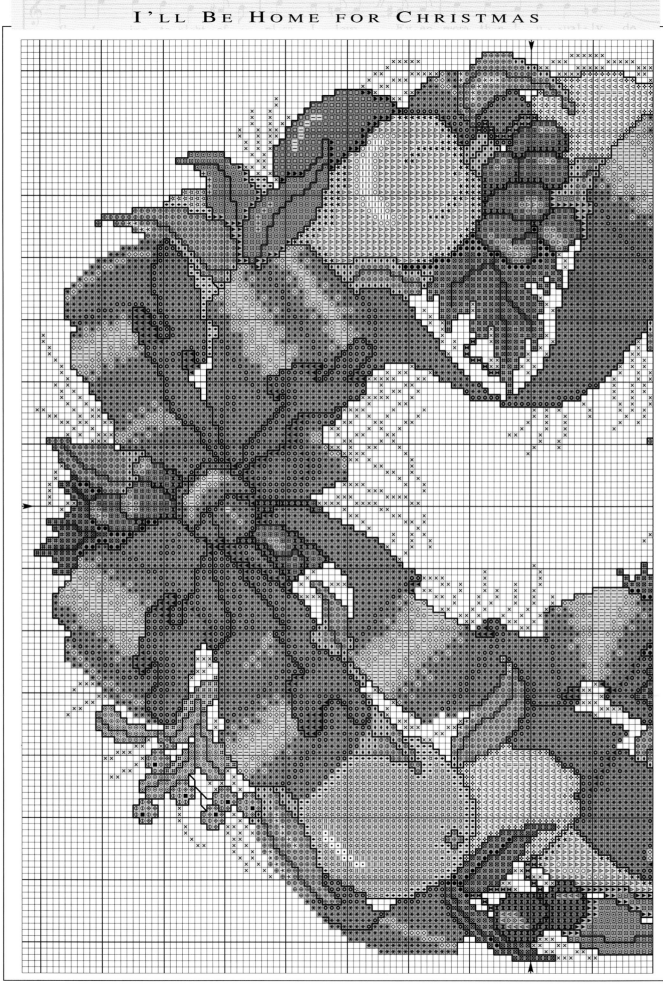

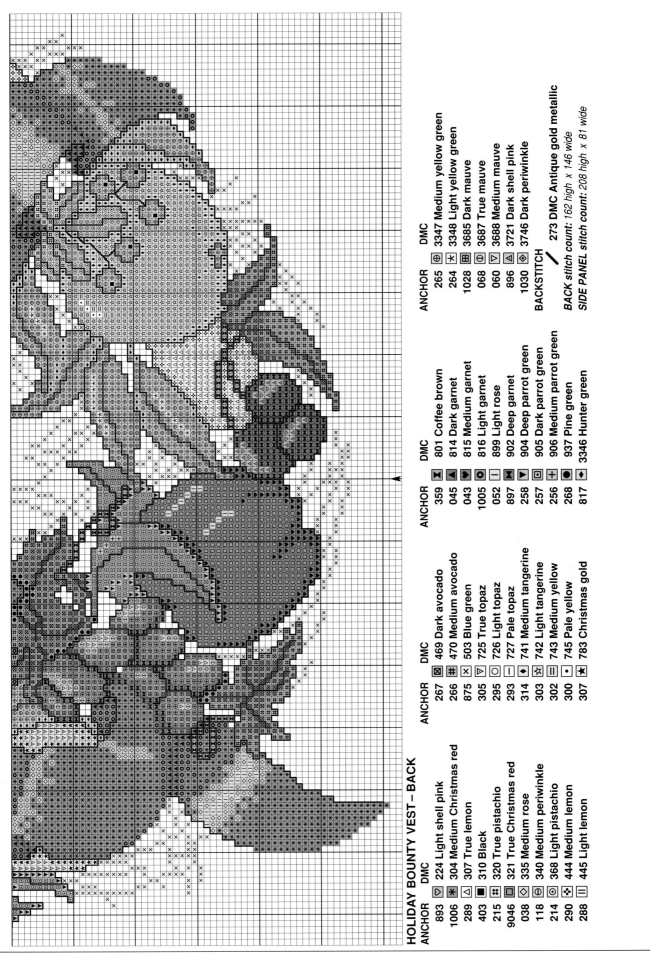

HOLIDAY BOUNTY VEST – BACK

ANCHOR		DMC	
893	▷	224	Light shell pink
1006	✱	304	Medium Christmas red
289	◁	307	True lemon
403	■	310	Black
215	⬚	320	True pistachio
9046	☐	321	True Christmas red
038	◇	335	Medium rose
118	⊕	340	Medium periwinkle
214	⊙	368	Light pistachio
290	✛	444	Medium lemon
288	‖	445	Light lemon

ANCHOR		DMC	
267	⊠	469	Dark avocado
266	#	470	Medium avocado
875	✕	503	Blue green
305	▷	725	True topaz
295	○	726	Light topaz
293	—	727	Pale topaz
314	◆	741	Medium tangerine
303	✬	742	Light tangerine
302	‖	743	Medium yellow
300	•	745	Pale yellow
307	✱	783	Christmas gold

ANCHOR		DMC	
359	✕	801	Coffee brown
045	◀	814	Dark garnet
043	▶	815	Medium garnet
1005	◐	816	Light garnet
052	—	899	Light rose
897	▶	902	Deep garnet
258	▶	904	Deep parrot green
257	⊡	905	Dark parrot green
256	+	906	Medium parrot green
268	●	937	Pine green
817	◆	3346	Hunter green

ANCHOR		DMC	
265	⊕	3347	Medium yellow green
264	✶	3348	Light yellow green
1028	⊞	3685	Dark mauve
068	⊖	3687	True mauve
060	▽	3688	Medium mauve
896	◣	3721	Dark shell pink
1030	◇	3746	Dark periwinkle

BACKSTITCH

273 DMC Antique gold metallic

BACK stitch count: 162 high x 146 wide
SIDE PANEL stitch count: 208 high x 81 wide

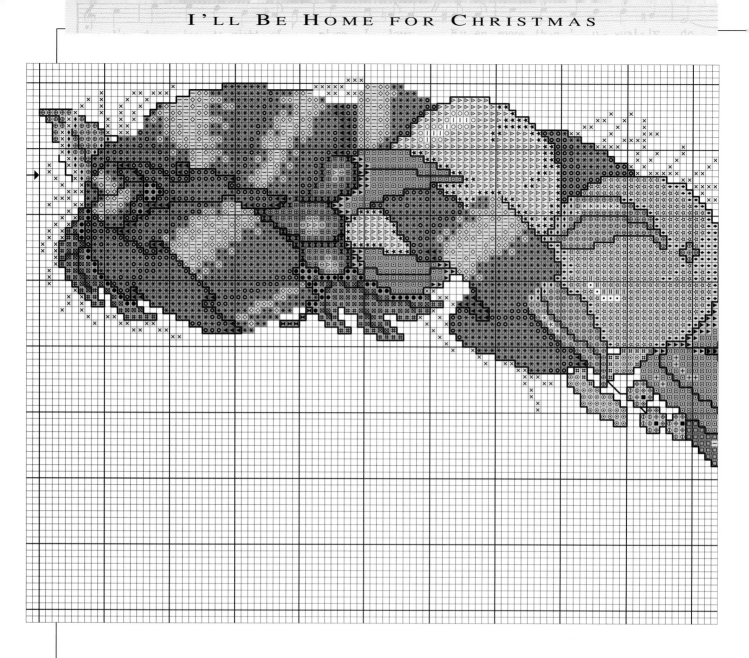

HOLIDAY BOUNTY VEST

Shown on page 9.

MATERIALS

FABRIC

54-inch-wide, 26-count navy
  Heatherfield fabric in amount
  specified on pattern envelope
Navy lining fabric in amount specified
  on pattern envelope (optional)

THREADS

Cotton embroidery floss in colors
  listed in key on page 19
Metallic embroidery thread in color
  listed in key on page 19

SUPPLIES

Purchased oversized vest pattern
Light-colored fabric marking pencil
Tapestry needle
Embroidery hoop
Notions as specified on pattern
  envelope; sewing thread

INSTRUCTIONS

Use fabric marking pen to trace
vest back, left front, and right front
outlines onto the Heatherfield fabric, allowing 2 inches between each
outline. Omit any pockets or pocket
flaps, but allow space for back ties
and facings if included in pattern.
Serge or zigzag the raw edges of
the fabric pieces to prevent fraying.

For back, measure 1⅝ inches
from neckline at center back.
Centering design from side to side,
begin stitching top row at center of
wreath chart, *pages 18–19,* there.
Work cross-stitches and backstitches using two plies of floss or one
strand of antique gold thread.

For left front (as worn), measure
2¾ inches, on straight grain, below
center of shoulder outline. Begin
stitching at arrow shown on chart,
above, working all stitches as for
vest back.

For right front, work as directed
for left front, *except* use chart on
pages 22–23.

Redraw vest outlines, if necessary. Cut out vest fronts, back, and
back ties, if included in pattern. Cut
out facings or lining, as specified in
pattern. Sew vest together following pattern directions.

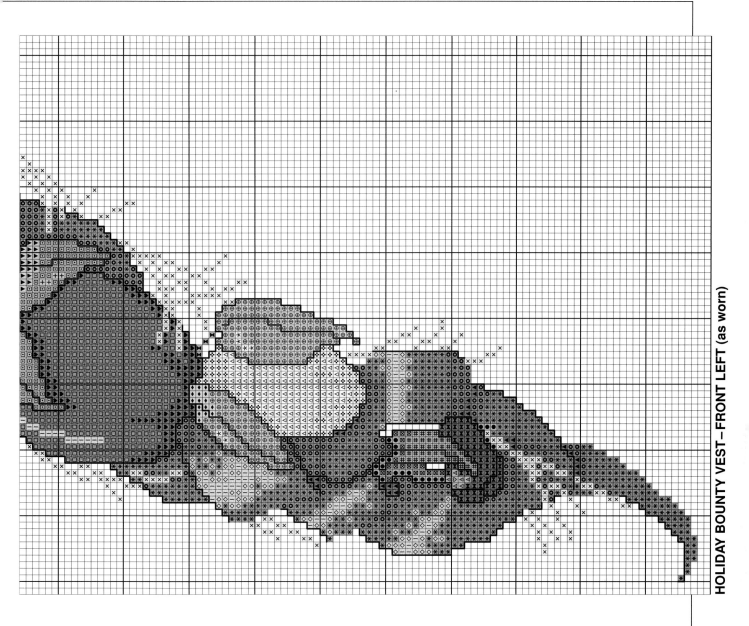

FRUIT AND MAGNOLIA FAN

As shown on page 10, fan measures approximately 12x41 inches.

MATERIALS

10x37-inch piece of ½-inch plywood
Band saw
Green paint and brush
20 eightpenny nails
6 tenpenny nails
Hammer
30 treated red or green magnolia
   leaves
One pineapple
20 red Delicious apples
12 feet of artificial greenery garland
Heavy-duty sawtooth hanger
Staple gun

INSTRUCTIONS

Draw a symmetrical arch shape on plywood measuring 10 inches high and 37 inches across bottom. Cut out the arch using a band saw. Paint the front of the arch green.

Begin at one bottom corner of the arch 2 inches from outer edge and hammer an eightpenny nail into the wood at a slight upward angle, leaving about 1½ inches of the nail exposed. Continue placing nails in same manner, each 4 to 5 inches apart, in a row around the curve of the arch. Measure 4 inches in from first row and make another curved row of nails. Make a third row of nails 4 inches in from second. Measure 2 inches from the bottom

center of arch. Hammer a tenpenny nail there and about 1 inch on either side to hold the pineapple. Hammer three more tenpenny nails about 3 inches above the first row.

Staple the magnolia leaves around the top of the arch with the ends extending approximately 3 inches past the edge. Begin at each bottom corner with the smallest leaves and work toward top with increasingly larger leaves. Reserve the largest leaves for the center.

Push an apple onto each eightpenny nail. Push the pineapple onto tenpenny nails in center. Twine greenery garland around the apples. Affix the hanger to the center back of the arch near the top.

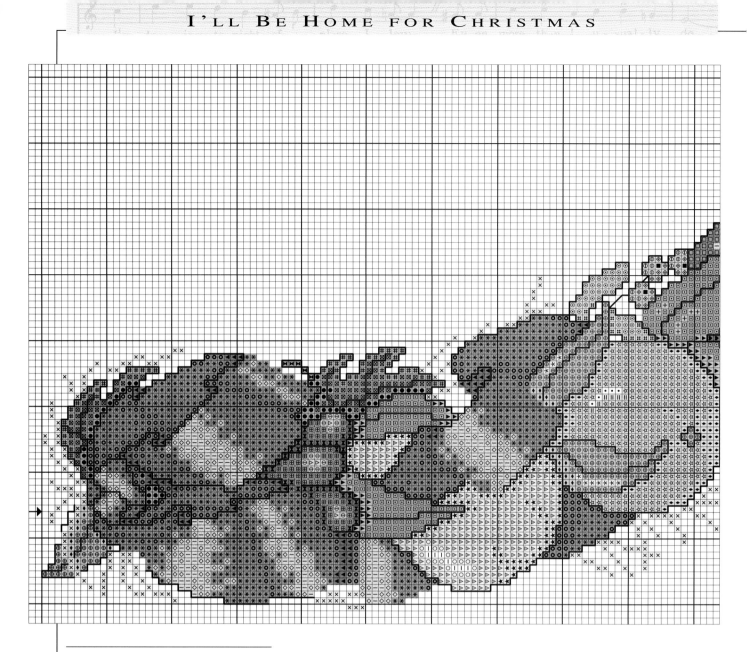

PEACHES AND GRAPES FLOORCLOTH

As shown on pages 10–11, floorcloth measures 24x36 inches.

MATERIALS
28x40-inch piece of heavy art canvas
Masking tape
T-square; yardstick; graphite pencil
Gesso; 3-inch soft bristle flat brush
Delta Ceramcoat paints: four bottles of midnight blue; one bottle each of ultra blue, bonnie blue, burnt umber, blue haze, pthalo green, white, napthol red light, AC flesh, mendocino, dark forest, burgundy rose, purple, black cherry, straw, and wedgwood green

Tracing paper
Small containers with lids for mixing
3- to 4-inch-diameter natural sponge
White pencil
White seral transfer paper
Graphite seral transfer paper
Crafts knife
Artist's brushes: small flat, medium flat, and #0 round
Styrofoam plates for palettes
Glue gun
Spray polyurethane varnish

INSTRUCTIONS
Tape canvas to a large rectangular work surface. Draw a 24x36-inch rectangle in the center of the canvas using a pencil. Paint the canvas with gesso, extending the gesso ¼ inch outside the pencil lines. Allow

the gesso to dry and apply a second coat. Cover the gesso with two coats of midnight blue, allowing the paint to dry between coats.

Meanwhile, trace the center design pattern, *pages 24–25,* onto tracing paper, joining left and right sections along fine dashed line. Also trace grape and leaf design and grape leaf border design patterns, *page 25.* Set patterns aside.

Pour one-half bottle of midnight blue into a small container and add two squirts each of ultra blue and bonnie blue. Mix well. Dip the sponge into the mixture and dab lightly onto newspaper to remove excess paint. Sponge the mixture over the floorcloth, allowing some midnight blue to show through.

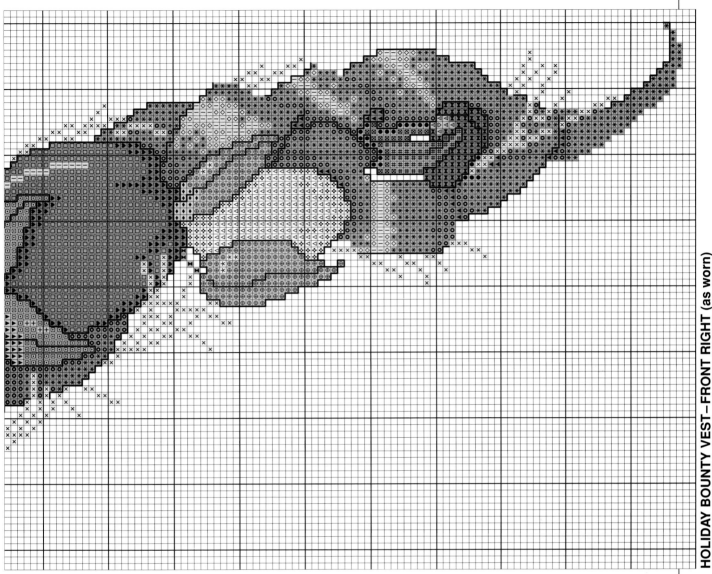

Redraw the floorcloth rectangle using the white pencil. Draw a second rectangle inside the first, 2½ inches away from all sides. In the same manner, draw a third rectangle 1¼ inches inside the second and a fourth rectangle ¼ inch inside the third. Referring to the diagram, *page 26,* draw lines every ½ inch across each side of the 2½-inch-wide outer border, leaving the corner squares unmarked. At each corner of the 1¼-inch-wide border, draw lines 1½ inches away from the corner to make the notched squares.

Mix equal parts burnt umber, midnight blue, and blue haze to make brown. Paint every other stripe and square around the outer border with the brown mixture.

Reserve the remainder of the brown for painting vines. Paint the middle border midnight blue, leaving the corner squares unpainted. Mix one part ultra blue, two parts pthalo green, and a small amount of white to make turquoise. Paint inner border turquoise. Reserve the remainder of the turquoise for painting cherry leaves later. Paint the notched squares in the middle border with several coats of napthol red light.

Use white seral paper to transfer 14 grape leaf designs to each lengthwise middle border and eight to each crosswise border. To space leaves evenly, begin positioning first leaf of each border about ¼ inch from notched square and allow

½ inch between leaves. Paint leaves blue haze. Paint the leaf veins using AC flesh and a #0 round brush.

Use a white pencil to mark the center of the rug with a cross. Position the center design pattern on the floorcloth with the pattern in the upper left quadrant of the design area and the cross at the center. Transfer the design using white seral paper. Flip the pattern over along the *dotted* line into the upper right quadrant to transfer the second quarter, omitting leaves, cherries, and vines marked with *. Flip the pattern over (back to the front side) along the *dashed* line and transfer the entire pattern to the lower right quadrant. To complete

Continued on page 25

CENTER DESIGN

the design, flip the pattern along the dotted line into the lower left quadrant and transfer omitting items marked with *. If desired, alter the pattern where the quarters meet, adding or subtracting leaves, or making cherries hang at different lengths on the stems.

Position the grape and leaf design pattern on the left side of one end of the floorcloth with the X centered 1⅝ inches inside the turquoise border. Transfer the design using white seral paper. Flip the pattern over along the dashed line to finish the transfer. Repeat for the other end.

For the grapes, base-paint with violet using a mixture of equal parts ultra blue and mendocino.

Mix AC flesh into dark forest to make olive. Working with one bunch of grapes at a time, choose four grapes at random from

Continued on page 27

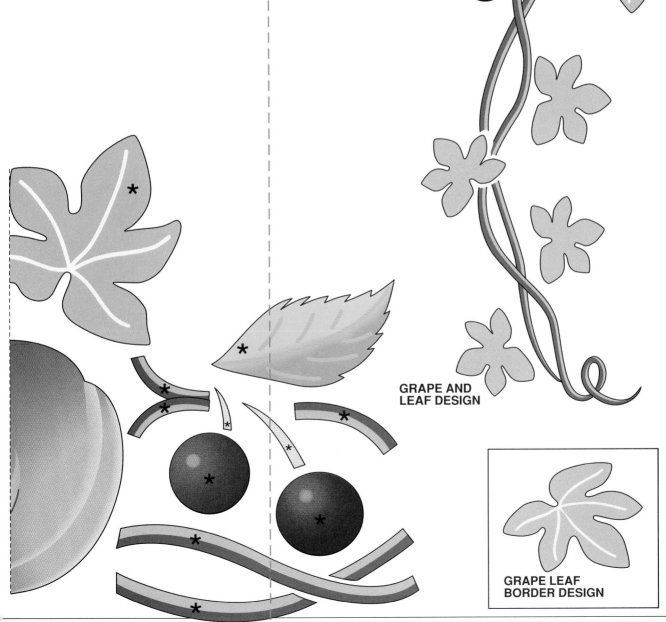

Center

GRAPE AND LEAF DESIGN

GRAPE LEAF BORDER DESIGN

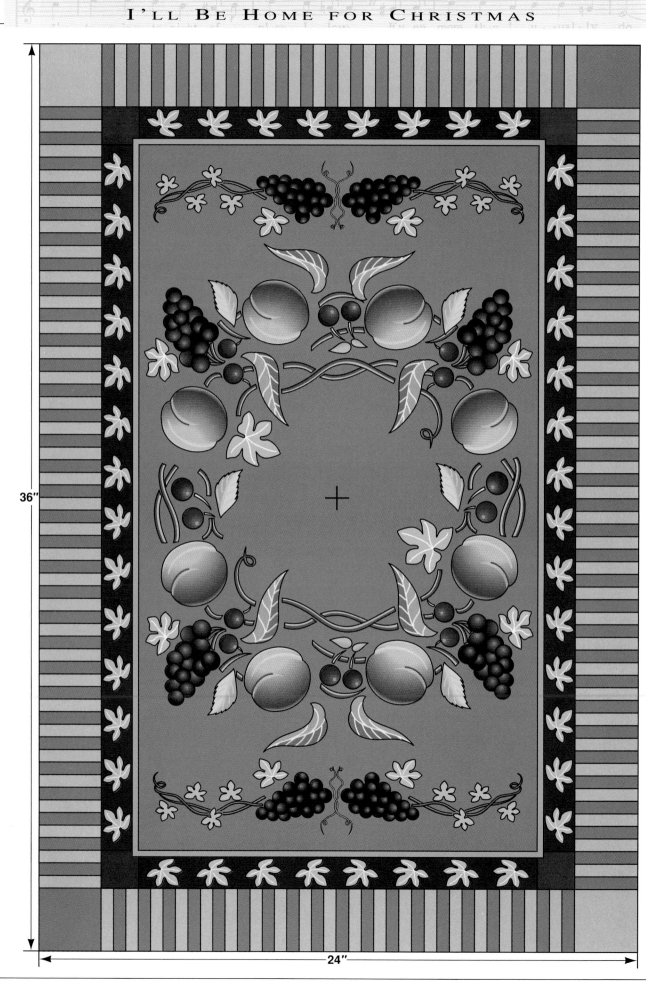

36"

24"

each bunch and brush olive around the outside of each. Mix burgundy rose with a little AC flesh and dry brush the mixture inside and over part of the olive, allowing some to show through. Dry-brush bonnie blue in the center, making small smudges of color. Shade using a mixture of burgundy rose, mendocino, and a small amount of purple. Highlight with AC flesh and a light pink from the palette.

Choose half of the remaining grapes at random and paint around half of the perimeter of each using a mixture of black cherry and midnight blue. Add AC flesh and dry-brush over parts of the grapes using circular strokes. Add more AC flesh and dry-brush in highlights. If desired, dab grapes with tiny smudges of bonnie blue.

Paint around the perimeters of the remaining grapes using a mixture of midnight blue and black cherry. Add more black cherry and brush inside the perimeters, blending the edges. Mix burgundy rose with black cherry, add a small amount of AC flesh, and dry-brush over some of the darker areas. Use a dabbing motion, allowing the previous colors to show through. Add a small amount of AC flesh to dark forest and dab the green on the edge of a couple of grapes. Dry-brush on top of the green using a mixture of bonnie blue and AC flesh. Highlight each grape with dots of AC flesh.

Fill in the background between the grapes in each bunch using a mixture of equal parts purple, midnight blue, and black cherry.

For the peaches, base-paint each with white. Mix two parts straw and one part napthol red light. Use this mixture to paint the peaches, beginning on the left side of each peach. Work across to the right, adding small amounts of napthol red light and using broad vertical brush strokes. Mix mendocino with a small amount of violet left from the grapes. Using a nearly dry brush, pull the red-violet down along the far right edge. Mix equal

parts burgundy rose and black cherry to paint the small triangle in the crease. Dry-brush AC flesh around the outside edge and lightly over the golden orange areas.

For cherries, base-paint each with white. Mix equal parts of mendocino and black cherry, and paint around the outside. Paint the center of each cherry napthol red light, blending with the darker color around the perimeter. Add white to the mixture to make pink and dry-brush a smudge slightly off center. Add more white and dry-brush a small highlight in the center of the pink smudge. Paint the stems AC flesh.

For the grape leaves in center and border, use blue haze. Brush in the vein lines using AC flesh.

For the peach leaves, base-paint with a mixture of equal parts wedgwood green and dark forest. Shade the folded leaves with dark forest. Shade the flat leaves using two parts dark forest to one part wedgwood green. For the lighter half of each flat leaf, use two parts wedgwood green to one part dark forest. Highlight all of the leaves and paint the veins using wedgwood green.

For cherry leaves, base-paint with blue haze. Mix some of the turquoise (left from the border) into blue haze. Use this mixture to paint the lighter half of each large leaf. Paint the darker half using turquoise mixed with a small amount of white. Shade the central vein using turquoise. Brush in the remaining veins using a mixture of two parts turquoise to one part white. Mix turquoise with a small amount of blue haze to paint the small cherry leaves.

For the grape vines, use the brown left from the outer border. Dry-brush blue haze along the vines for highlights.

Turn unpainted edges to the back, miter the corners, and glue in place. Spray the floorcloth with two coats of polyurethane varnish, allowing the first coat to dry before applying the second.

MIRROR PLACE CARDS

As shown on page 12, place cards each measure 2x4¼ inches.

MATERIALS
4¼-inch-diameter gold or silver doilies (each doily makes two place cards)
Medium weight red art paper
Acrylic mirrors: 28-millimeter squares, 40x30-millimeter ovals, and/or 40-millimeter rounds
12-millimeter-long red or gold acrylic navette-shaped stones
2-centimeter-long red or green acrylic holly leaf-shaped stones
6-millimeter red or green acrylic round stones (optional)
4-millimeter faceted gold beads
Rhinestone adhesive or crafts glue
Red paint pen

INSTRUCTIONS
Cut one doily in half and trim the straight edge of each of the halves so the piece measures 2 inches high. Reserve one half for a second place card.

For the square mirror design, cut a piece of red art paper 1¼x3⅛ inches and glue it to the back of the doily, aligning the bottom edges. Glue three square mirrors across the bottom of the doily, aligning the bottom edges.

Arrange and glue navettes and holly leaf-shaped stones to one of the mirror pieces to resemble a poinsettia and leaves. Use a round stone or faceted beads for flower center. Write a name across remaining mirrors using the paint pen.

For an oval or round mirror design, cut an arch-shaped piece of red art paper slightly smaller than the doily piece and glue it to the back of the doily, aligning the bottom edges. Glue an oval and round mirror to center of doily.

Arrange and glue navettes and holly leaves near the edges of the doily to resemble poinsettias and leaves. Use round stones or faceted beads for the flower centers. Write names on the mirrors using the paint pen.

POINSETTIA APPLIQUÉ SWEATER

Shown on page 13.

MATERIALS

FABRICS

**Light pink mock turtleneck
long-sleeved cotton sweater**

**6x16-inch piece of red felted
imitation suede (lower petals)**

**6x16-inch piece of pink felted
imitation suede (upper petals)**

**6x6-inch piece of green felted
imitation suede (leaves)**

**6x6-inch piece of turquoise felted
imitation suede (leaves)**

SUPPLIES

**16x18-inch piece of paper-backed
iron-on adhesive**

**Twenty-nine 5-millimeter pink or gold
metallic faceted beads**

**¼-inch frost green heart-shaped
beads**

Gold metallic sewing thread

Light pink sewing thread

Tracing paper

Press cloth

INSTRUCTIONS

Trace petals and leaves from pattern, *above* and *opposite,* separately onto tracing paper. Use solid black outlines for pink upper petals, dashed black outlines for red lower petals, solid green outlines for green leaves, and dashed green outlines for turquoise leaves. Cut out and mark patterns.

Trace around pattern pieces, front side down, on paper side of iron-on adhesive; cut out. Fuse to wrong side of corresponding colors of imitation suede following manufacturer's instructions. Cut out.

Remove paper from iron-on adhesive. Arrange all imitation suede pieces in place on sweater, positioning top center of design 1 inch below neck ribbing. Set pink and red petals aside. Place press cloth over leaves and fuse in place following manufacturer's instructions. Place red petals atop leaves, cover with press cloth, and fuse. Place pink petals in place, cover with press cloth, and fuse.

Work a machine zigzag-appliqué stitch around edges of petals and leaves using gold thread in needle and pink thread in bobbin. Stitch leaf center veins in same manner.

Sew faceted beads at small circles in flower centers. Sew heart-shaped beads in lines of three randomly around flowers.

CREAMY CARAMEL-PECAN ROLLS

Shown on page 15.

INGREDIENTS

1¼ cups sifted powdered sugar
½ cup whipping cream
1 cup coarsely chopped pecans
2 14- to 16-ounce loaves frozen sweet or white bread dough, thawed
3 tablespoons margarine or butter, melted
½ cup packed brown sugar
1 tablespoon ground cinnamon

METHOD

For topping, in a small mixing bowl stir together powdered sugar and whipping cream. Divide evenly between two 9x1½-inch round baking pans. Sprinkle pecans evenly over sugar mixture.

Roll each loaf of dough into a 12x8-inch rectangle on a lightly floured surface. Brush with melted margarine or butter. In a small mixing bowl stir together brown sugar and cinnamon; sprinkle over dough. Roll up rectangles, jelly-roll style, starting from a long side. Pinch to seal. Cut each into 10 to 12 slices.

Place rolls, cut side down atop pecan mixture. Cover with a warm towel. Let rise in a warm place until nearly double, about 30 minutes. (Or, cover with oiled waxed paper, then with plastic wrap. Refrigerate 2 to 24 hours. Before baking, let chilled rolls stand, covered, 20 minutes at room temperature. Puncture any surface bubbles with a greased toothpick.)

Bake rolls, uncovered, in a 375° oven till golden allowing 20 to 25 minutes for unchilled rolls and 25 to 30 minutes for chilled rolls. If necessary, cover rolls with foil the last 10 minutes to prevent overbrowning. Cool in pans 5 minutes on a wire rack. Invert onto a serving platter. Serve warm. Makes 20 to 24 rolls.

KISSING BALL

As shown on page 16, the finished ball measures 7 inches in diameter.

MATERIALS

One orange
Small heart-shaped cookie cutter
Ten strands of raffia
Small piece of florist's wire
Hot glue gun
One 6-inch-diameter open grapevine ball form
Spanish moss
Eight large artificial ivory berries
Seven preserved red myrtle leaves
Five pieces of light green reindeer moss
Five silk burgundy ivy leaves
One cinnamon stick, broken into pieces
Small bunch of sweet Annie
Hawthorne berries
Oregano blossoms
Greenery clippers or scissors

INSTRUCTIONS

For orange peel hearts, cut a piece out of the top of the orange and scoop out the pulp. Slitting the peel as little as necessary, lay it flat on a work surface. Use the heart-shaped cookie cutter to cut four or five small heart shapes from the orange peel. Allow the hearts to dry overnight.

Fill the grapevine ball with Spanish moss. Pull a few small bits of moss out through the holes in the wreath at random.

Tie six of the raffia strands in a bow approximately four inches across. Wire the bow to the top of the ball. Knot a strand of raffia at the center of the bow to make a hanging loop. Glue the remaining raffia strands to the bottom of the ball to make streamers.

Hang the ball over the work surface. Hot-glue the orange peel hearts and remaining materials to the ball at random, spacing each type of material evenly around the ball. Leave small areas of the ball exposed and save a few small items to glue to the raffia streamers.

SERENDIPITY WREATH

As shown on page 17, wreath measures 17 inches in diameter.

MATERIALS

15-inch-diameter spring clamp wire wreath form
Spanish moss
Large bunch of treated sweet Annie
Hot glue gun
Three dried baby pomegranates
Five dried quince slices
Two dried artichokes
One stem of silk burgundy ivy
Five cedar roses
Ten pieces of light green reindeer moss
One large burgundy cockscomb
Twelve dried clusters of hawthorne berries
Four dried apple slices
Four small bunches of Queen Anne's lace
Three cinnamon sticks, broken in half
Three stems of oregano
One stem of mountain mint
Small twigs
Green and red preserved myrtle
Ivory canella berries
Three pheasant feathers, cut in half
Twelve strands of raffia
Two stems of small artificial ivory berries
Artificial burgundy berries
Greenery clippers or scissors

INSTRUCTIONS

Open the clamps on wreath form and fill the form with Spanish moss. Arrange treated sweet Annie around Spanish moss, allowing it to extend beyond the edges of the form. Fold the clamps over to secure both Spanish moss and sweet Annie.

Hot-glue the remaining materials to the wreath beginning with pomegranates, quinces, and artichokes. Space each type of material evenly around wreath for a balanced appearance. Next, add the silk ivy, cedar roses, moss, and cockscomb. Glue in rest of materials, leaving the feathers, raffia strands, and artificial berries for last.

Deck the Halls

Deck the halls with boughs of holly and the delightful crafts we've showcased in this chapter. We've created a festive array of projects that you can make to decorate your home for the holidays. Whether it is a quick-to-make sparkling candle, an elegant satin yo-yo stocking, or a lovable stuffed red teddy bear—these heartwarming treasures will fill your home with the spirit of the season.

PHOTOGRAPHER: HOPKINS ASSOCIATES

Yo-yo Stocking

Old-fashioned yo-yos dressed up in fancy fabrics and buttons adorn this rich velvet stocking. Hang it from your mantel early in the season so you can enjoy its elegance long before Santa's visit. Instructions and patterns are on page 40.

Golden Fruit Centerpiece

Create this rich golden centerpiece to enhance your most elegant gatherings, year after year. Plastic fruit is spray painted, arranged, and glued in place for a truly stunning effect. Instructions begin on page 41.

DESIGNERS: STOCKING, MARGARET SINDELAR; CENTERPIECE, GERRY BAUMAN
PHOTOGRAPHER: STOCKING, HOPKINS ASSOCIATES; CENTERPIECE, SCOTT LITTLE

Noah's Ark and Holiday Bell Edging Scherenschnitte

Snipped with patient and loving hands, our framed Noah's Ark scherenschnitte makes a favorite family keepsake or a heartfelt gift. You may wish to make two—one to give and one to keep. Add a festive touch to a library or family room by adorning shelves with paper cut-out garlands. Use tiny scissors and white paper to produce the delightful lacy effect. Instructions and patterns for both projects begin on page 47.

DESIGNER: LINDA ARTHUR ● PHOTOGRAPHER: HOPKINS ASSOCIATES

Jolly Santa and Tree Candleholder

This jolly Santa and Christmas tree candleholder, charmingly rendered in wood and paint, is sure to become a special part of your holiday celebration. The figures are grouped on a large oval base to set a merry mood wherever the candleholder is placed. Instructions and patterns begin on page 48.

DESIGNER: HELEN NICHOLSON ● PHOTOGRAPHER: SCOTT LITTLE

Cardinal Afghan

Snuggle up in front of the fireplace in this cozy holiday afghan. Cardinals, long a symbol of the winter season, offer striking contrast to a soft charcoal background. Knit this afghan all in one piece and add small duplicate-stitch details last. Instructions and chart are on pages 51–52.

DESIGNER: VALERIE ROOT ● PHOTOGRAPHER: HOPKINS ASSOCIATES

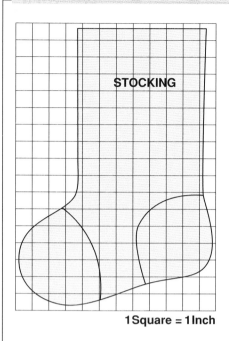

STOCKING

1 Square = 1 Inch

YO-YO STOCKING

As shown on page 35, stocking measures 16½ inches long.

MATERIALS

FABRICS

⅔ yard of 45-inch-wide deep-red velveteen fabric

15x20-inch piece of fleece

½ yard of 45-inch-wide deep-red moiré taffeta

½ yard of 45-inch-wide red lining fabric

Small pieces of assorted shades of red, burgundy, violet, green, and pink

SUPPLIES

Graph paper

Tracing paper

Fabric marking pen

2 yards of narrow cording

Threads to match fabrics

¾ yard of ½-inch-wide flat antique gold trim

50 fancy shank buttons, measuring ⅜- to ¾-inch in diameter

¾ yard of 3-inch-wide scalloped antique gold trim

Two yards of ³⁄₁₆-inch-diameter metallic gold cord

INSTRUCTIONS

Sew all pieces with right sides of fabric facing and clip curves. Patterns and measurements include ¼-inch seam allowances.

For stocking front, cut a 15x20-inch piece of velveteen. Baste fleece to back side of velveteen and machine-quilt using a 1-inch diagonal grid diamond pattern.

Enlarge stocking pattern, *left,* onto graph paper and trace yo-yo circles, *below,* onto tracing paper. Cut out pattern pieces.

Cut stocking front from quilted fabric. Transfer heel and toe lines. From unquilted velveteen, cut a 5½x16-inch cuff, a 2x5½-inch hanging loop, and enough 1-inch-wide bias strips to make 2 yards. Cut stocking back from taffeta. Cut two lining pieces and a 5½x16-inch cuff lining from lining fabric. From assorted pieces of taffeta, cut 25 large and 25 small circles.

For yo-yos, turn under a scant ¼ inch around perimeter of each yo-yo circle and finger-press. Gather outside folded edge of each circle using a running stitch. Pull the gathers tight, knot the thread, and flatten into a circle with gathers in center.

Stitch ½-inch-wide gold trim to toe and heel lines on stocking front.

For piping, sew bias velveteen strips end to end. Center cording lengthwise on wrong side of velveteen strip. Fold fabric around

cording, raw edges together. Use a zipper foot to sew through both layers, close to cord. Trim seam allowance to ¼ inch. Baste piping around stocking front along side and bottom edges. Sew stocking front to back, leaving top open. Turn right side out.

Sew 11 yo-yos, gathered side up, to toe, securing center of each with a button and positioning yo-yos close together with overlapping edges. Sew 12 yo-yos to heel in same manner.

Join short ends of velveteen cuff strip. Repeat for cuff lining. Stitch velveteen cuff to cuff lining around one long edge (bottom). Turn cuff right side out and stitch 3-inch-wide trim to bottom. Baste cuff to stocking top, matching raw edges.

Turn under ½ inch along long sides of hanging loop strip. Fold strip in half lengthwise and stitch close to folded edges. Fold strip in half crosswise to form a loop; matching short ends to raw edge, stitch loop to cuff at back seam.

Sew lining front to back, leaving top open and an opening at bottom for turning. Slip stocking into lining with right sides facing, matching seams. Stitch around top edge. Turn right side out through bottom

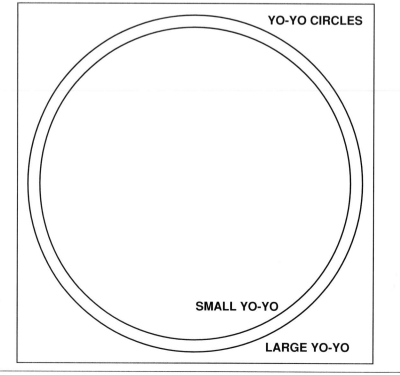

YO-YO CIRCLES

SMALL YO-YO

LARGE YO-YO

opening in lining and slip-stitch opening closed. Tuck lining into stocking and tack at seams.

Sew 27 yo-yos to cuff front, as for heel and toe. Cut gold cord length in half and knot ends. Tie cords in a double bow and stitch to cuff below hanging loop.

GOLDEN FRUIT CENTERPIECE

As shown on page 34, centerpiece measures approximately 27 inches long, 9 inches wide, and 9 inches tall.

MATERIALS

Two bunches of artificial grapes
One artificial pineapple
Three artificial apples
Three artificial pears
Three artificial pomegranates
Three artificial oranges
Two artificial lemons
Artificial raspberries
Gold metallic spray paint
14-inch-diameter wire clamp ring wreath form
Wire cutters; florist's wire
Spanish moss
Real or artificial greenery
Hot-glue gun; florist's tape
Two yards of burgundy and gold cord
Two burgundy candles in short candleholders

INSTRUCTIONS

Cut grapes into small bunches. Spray all fruit, *except* raspberries, with gold paint and allow to dry. Cut wreath form in half using wire cutters. Join two half-circles with florist's wire to make an S shape. Fill form with Spanish moss and a thin layer of greenery. Secure pineapple to center of S shape using hot glue and florist's tape as needed. Glue and tape remaining fruit along form, tucking grape bunches into spaces between larger fruit. When complete, spray entire centerpiece with gold paint to cover any visible tape or areas where paint has been removed.

Tuck sprigs of raspberries into centerpiece at random. Twine cord loosely among fruit. Arrange centerpiece on top of additional greenery. Position candles in curves.

SPARKLING CANDLES

Shown on page 36.

MATERIALS

Tracing paper
Pencil
Four 6-inch-tall plain pillar candles
Masking tape; tapestry needle
One hundred and seventy ¼-inch-diameter gold nailhead studs
One ⅝-inch gold star-shaped stud
Gold metallic paint marker
Thirteen ⅜-inch-diameter gold nailhead studs

INSTRUCTIONS

For starburst design (shown on green candle), fold a 4½-inch square of tracing paper in half. Aligning the fold with the dotted line on the pattern, trace starburst pattern, *below*. Turn the folded

tracing paper over and trace pattern on the opposite side of the fold; unfold. Center pattern on candle and tape. With needle, make a small hole in the center of each paper circle and a light indentation on the candle. Remove pattern and press ¼-inch studs into candle at each indentation. Press star-shaped stud into center.

For large snowflake design (shown on red candle), fold a 4½-inch square of tracing paper in half; repeat bringing folded edges together. Matching folds, trace

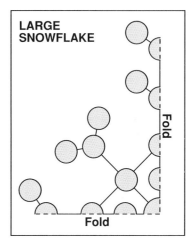

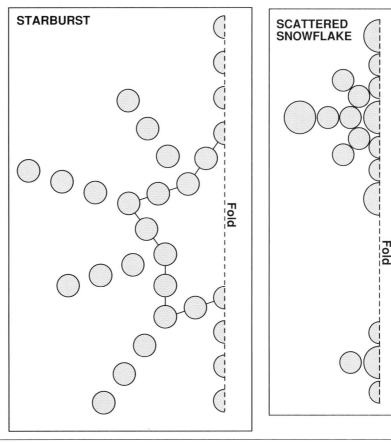

pattern, *page 41,* onto tracing paper. Turn folded tracing paper over and trace pattern on opposite side of fold; unfold once and trace pattern on remaining two quarters of paper. Unfold pattern; tape to candle, centering from top to bottom. Trace lines and make indentations for stud placement with needle. Remove pattern and draw over lines using gold marker. Press a ⅜-inch stud into center and ¼-inch studs into remaining indentations.

For scattered snowflake design (shown on white candles), fold 4½-inch square of tracing paper in half. Align fold with dotted line on pattern, *page 41;* trace. Turn folded tracing paper over and trace pattern on opposite side of fold; unfold. Center pattern on candle and tape. With needle, make a small hole in center of each paper circle and a light indentation on candle. Remove pattern and press ⅜-inch and ¼-inch studs into appropriate positions as shown on pattern.

WINTER FROST SAMPLER

As shown on page 35, sampler measures 17x13 inches.

MATERIALS

FABRIC
24x18-inch piece of 28-count ecru linen

THREADS
Cotton embroidery floss in colors listed in key
#8 braid in color listed in key

SUPPLIES
Needle; embroidery hoop
Desired frame and mat

INSTRUCTIONS

Tape or zigzag edges of fabric to prevent fraying. Find center of chart and of fabric; begin stitching there. Use two plies of floss or one strand of braid to work cross-stitches over two threads of fabric. Use one ply to work backstitches.

Press finished stitchery on wrong side with a cool iron. Frame and mat as desired.

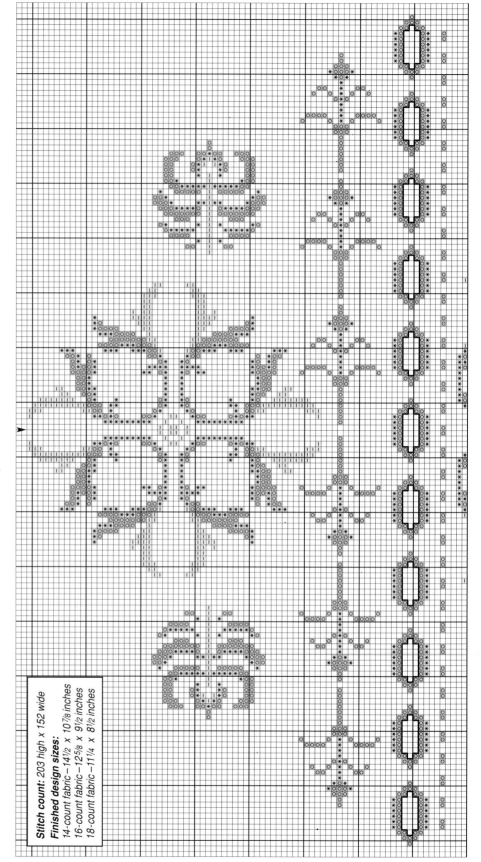

Stitch count: 203 high x 152 wide
Finished design sizes:
14-count fabric – 14½ x 10⅞ inches
16-count fabric – 12⅝ x 9½ inches
18-count fabric – 11¼ x 8½ inches

WINTER FROST SAMPLER

ANCHOR	DMC	ANCHOR	DMC
1045 ◎ 436 Dark tan		362 ⊟ 437 Medium tan	

ANCHOR	DMC
✳ 221 Kreinik antique gold #8 braid	

ANCHOR	DMC
BACKSTITCH	
362 ╱ 437 Medium tan	

BUTTONS THE BEAR

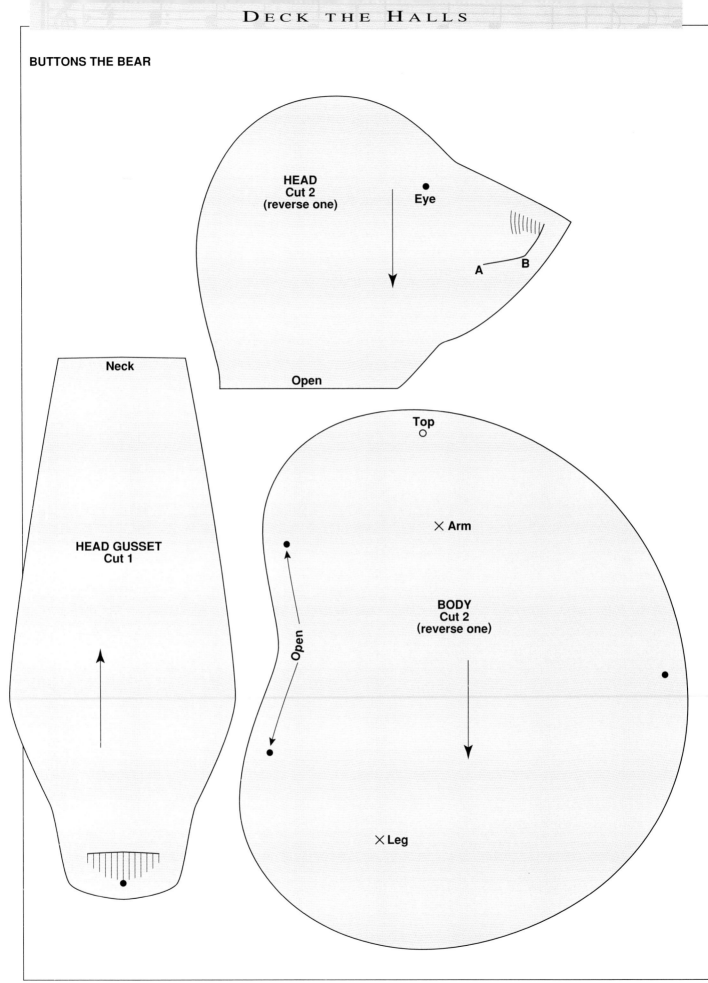

HEAD
Cut 2
(reverse one)

Eye

A   B

Neck

Open

Top

HEAD GUSSET
Cut 1

✕ Arm

BODY
Cut 2
(reverse one)

Open

✕ Leg

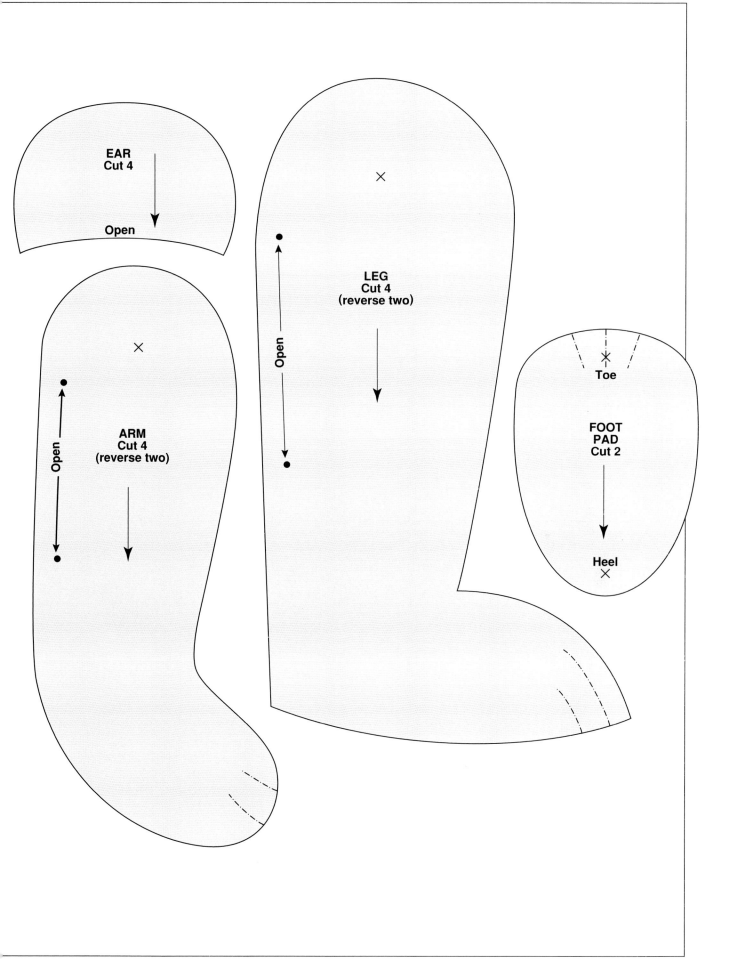

EAR
Cut 4

Open

LEG
Cut 4
(reverse two)

Open

ARM
Cut 4
(reverse two)

Open

Toe

FOOT
PAD
Cut 2

Heel

45

BUTTONS THE BEAR

As shown on page 36, bear stands 12 inches tall.

MATERIALS

FABRIC
¼ yard of Alfonso red mohair (red pile on a cream backing) with ⅜-inch-long pile

THREADS
Cream sewing thread
Red sewing thread
Red carpet thread
#3 black pearl cotton

SUPPLIES
Tissue paper
Thin cardboard
Fabric marking pen
Scissors
Large-eyed embroidery or leather needle
Beeswax
One 1x¼-inch bolt
Two 1-inch-diameter fiberboard disks with ¼-inch-diameter holes
T-pins
Awl
Soft-sculpture needle
Two 8-millimeter antique shoe eye buttons
One ¼-inch lock washer
One ¼-inch nut
Needle-nose pliers
Polyester fiberfill
⅓ yard of 1½-inch-wide ecru cotton lace
Fifteen assorted antique pearl buttons
Leather thimble
Chopstick or small dowel

INSTRUCTIONS

Trace pattern, *pages 44–45,* onto tissue paper and cut out. Draw around pieces on cardboard and cut out to make templates. All patterns include ¼-inch seam allowances. Sew all seams with right sides facing, unless otherwise noted.

Place pattern templates on wrong side of a single thickness of mohair, positioning each piece so arrow runs in direction of nap. Trace around templates, reversing pieces where indicated. Using fabric marking pen, transfer pattern markings. Cut out fabric pieces using tip of scissors to snip through fabric backing and being careful not to cut pile on right side.

For head, join head side pieces along chin seam from neck front to nose. Hand-baste gusset between head pieces, matching dot to top of chin seam. Machine-stitch gusset in place. Remove basting threads, clip curves, and turn head right side out. Stuff head firmly. Thread large-eyed needle with a double strand of carpet thread. Knot thread ends and rub strands with beeswax. Work a running stitch around neck, allowing needle and thread to hang from last stitch. Insert bolt through hole in one disk. Push disk into neck opening with bottom of bolt extending below opening. Pull carpet thread to gather neck around bolt. Knot thread securely.

Sew ears together in pairs leaving bottoms open. Turn ears right side out. Turn under ¼ inch along ear bottom edges and slip-stitch closed. With upper edge of each ear on head gusset seamline, pin ears to head using T-pins. When ears are positioned as desired, stitch them in place using carpet thread.

For eyes, use awl to punch a hole at each eye position. Thread soft-sculpture needle with four strands of carpet thread and knot ends around wire loop of one eye button. Push needle into one eye hole, exiting behind ear on opposite side of head. Pull thread tight to sink eye in hole and knot thread. Repeat for remaining eye.

Trim away as much pile as possible on nose where it will be embroidered. Trim a scant ⅛ inch from pile on remainder of muzzle. Straight-stitch nose and claws, as shown on pattern, *pages 44–45,* using large-eyed needle and a single strand of pearl cotton. To make mouth, use a single strand of pearl cotton knotted at end. Hide knot behind embroidered nose and push needle out through point A on left side. Leaving stitch loose, push needle into face at point A on right side and out at point B. Bring the needle under the loose stitch and pull to tighten, creating an inverted 'V' for mouth. Push the needle back into the face at base of the nose and knot thread.

For arms and legs, sew pieces together in pairs leaving marked openings unstitched. Sew a foot pad to each foot bottom, matching toe and heel Xs to front and back seams. Turn limbs right side out.

For body, sew sides together, leaving marked openings unstitched. Turn body right side out. Make a hole at dot on body top using awl. Push bolt end that extends from head into body through hole. Entering from body back opening, slide remaining disk and lock washer onto bolt; secure both with nut. Tighten nut using pliers until head just barely turns.

Stuff arms, legs, and body firmly. Sew openings closed with a double strand of carpet thread coated with beeswax. Next, thread soft-sculpture needle with a double strand of carpet thread and knot ends. Sew arms to body by pushing needle through one arm at Xs, through body at Xs, and then through remaining arm at Xs. Pull thread tight and sew back through in opposite direction, exiting near starting point. Slide a button onto thread and push needle back through to outside of other arm. Slide another button onto thread and sew through again, exiting through one of holes in button. Continue sewing back and forth in same manner four more times, securing buttons while stitching. Knot thread on inside of one arm. Sew legs to body in same manner.

Tie lace in a bow around neck and trim ends. Using assorted pearl buttons, sew smallest button in right ear, a large button to middle of bow, a small button at dot on tummy, a small button to outside of each wrist to resemble cuff buttons, and three buttons up the side of each leg to resemble spat buttons.

Smooth pile away from eyes using a finger dipped in water or styling mousse.

HOLIDAY BELL EDGING

To finish, press cutting on the pencil-traced (wrong) side with a warm iron. Secure top edge to shelf with small pieces of tape.

NOAH'S ARK SCHERENSCHNITTE

As shown on page 37, actual cut design measures 8¾x7¾ inches.

MATERIALS
#2 pencil
Tracing paper
8x10-inch piece of white paper
Cellophane tape
Teaspoon
Scherenschnitte scissors or crafts knife and cutting mat or old magazine
White crafts glue
8x10-inch piece of contrasting background paper

INSTRUCTIONS
Trace pattern, *page 48,* onto tracing paper, using #2 pencil. Fold white paper in half lengthwise and secure open edges together with small pieces of tape. Place pencil-sketched side of tracing paper atop folded paper with dashed line along fold. Using rim of teaspoon, stroke firmly along pencil lines until all of image, except Noah and his wife, is transferred. (They will be transferred and cut after other cutting is finished.)

To cut design, first poke holes through eye dots on birds and animals using pin. Then, use scherenschnitte scissors to cut away inside areas through both layers. (Or, tape edges of paper to cutting mat and use crafts knife.) Cut around outside edges last. Unfold paper. Transfer cutting lines for Noah figures onto back of paper and cut out.

To finish, press cutting on the pencil-traced (wrong) side with a warm iron. Place tiny dabs of glue at various points on wrong side of cutting and position it atop background paper, smoothing the two pieces together. Frame as desired.

HOLIDAY BELL EDGING
As shown on page 37, each motif measures 3x5⅞ inches, plus a 1-inch-wide top strip.

MATERIALS
#2 pencil
Tracing paper
4-inch-wide strip of white paper, cut to desired length
Teaspoon
Pin
Scherenschnitte scissors or crafts knife and cutting mat or old magazine
Cellophane tape

INSTRUCTIONS
Trace pattern, *above,* onto tracing paper, using pencil. Aligning side edges, trace as many repeat patterns as neccessary for desired length. Place pencil-sketched side of tracing paper atop white paper strip, aligning top and left edges. Using rim of teaspoon, stroke firmly along pencil lines until complete image is transferred. Fold top edge of paper strip, crease, and unfold.

To cut design, first poke holes through eye dots on birds using pin. Then, use scherenschnitte scissors to cut away inside areas. (Or, tape edges of paper to cutting mat and use crafts knife.) Cut around outside edge last.

NOAH'S ARK

JOLLY SANTA AND TREE CANDLEHOLDER

As shown on page 38, finished candleholder is 9¼ inches tall.

MATERIALS
Tracing paper
12x12-inch piece of ⅜-inch birch plywood
10x6-inch piece of 1-inch pine
Bandsaw
Router
150 grit sandpaper
Tack cloth
Folkart acrylic paints: antique gold metallic, barnyard red, burnt umber, country twill, heartland blue, licorice, nutmeg, peach cobbler, plantation green, sunny yellow, wicker white, and wrought iron
Transfer paper
Pencil
#6 and #8 flat brushes
#1 round brush
#1 liner brush
Old #6 flat brush with scruffy-looking bristles
Ultra-fine-point technical pen
Stylus; old toothbrush
Unfinished wood candle cup
Gold glitter paint pen
Satin-finish waterbase varnish
Hot glue gun
Drill with ⅛-inch and countersink bit
Five 6x1¼ flathead Phillips wood screws
One 6x¾ flathead Phillips wood screw
Phillips screw driver

INSTRUCTIONS
Trace tree, star, Santa, and bear patterns, *pages 49–50,* onto tracing paper, and cut out. Draw around tree, star, bear, and Santa outlines on plywood. Enlarge base pattern, *page 50,* and cut out. Draw around base outline on pine. Cut out pieces using a bandsaw. Router top edge of base as desired. Sand all pieces and wipe with a tack cloth.

Coat front and edges of Santa, tree, star, and bear with a wash of wicker white. Sand lightly and wipe with a tack cloth. Paint back of same pieces with two coats of licorice, sanding lightly between coats. Using transfer paper and a pencil, transfer detail from patterns to appropriate wood pieces.

To paint, thin paints with water to acheive a soft look while painting. Use a #8 flat brush for base-coating, a #1 round brush for filling in small areas and for larger details, and a #1 liner brush for applying small details. Add eyelashes and similar tiny lines using a black technical pen. Use handle tip of a #1 liner brush to paint larger dots and stylus for smaller dots. Allow each paint application to dry before beginning another.

To float paint, dampen a #6 flat brush with water, side-load, and blend on palette using S strokes. Paint, keeping edge of brush with greatest amount of paint along area requiring greatest intensity of color.

For star, base-coat twice with antique gold metallic, sanding between coats. Add tiny stars using liner brush and thinned wicker white. Dot perimeter using stylus dipped in wicker white.

For tree, pour a puddle of plantation green the size of a half-dollar onto palette. Add one teaspoon of water and mix well. Apply resulting wash to tree branches using #8 flat brush. Paint trunk and basket with a wash of nutmeg. To begin shading, float plantation green over tree branches, referring to pattern for areas of deepest color. Deepen shading with wrought iron. Highlight with plantation green. Highlight edges of a few branches once again using a wash of wicker white. Shade trunk and basket with burnt umber. Detail basket using licorice and highlight with a float of wicker white.

For tree's ornaments, base-coat with wicker white. Refer to pattern, *right,* for ornament colors. For barnyard red and heartland blue ornaments, float paint around each ornament, allowing a small amount of white to show through. Base-coat remaining ornaments sunny yellow and shade with nutmeg. Highlight each ornament with a stroke of wicker white. Dot garland using liner brush handle dipped in wicker white.

For Santa's hat, coat, and pants, coat each with a wash of barnyard red. Highlight with a wash of sunny yellow. Next, float barnyard red around fur and in folds. Using stylus, add tiny dots of wicker white to hat and pants. Using liner brush and thinned wicker white, add tiny stars to hat and pants between dots.

For Santa's fur, first float edges with country twill. Deepen shading with burnt umber. When dry, dip tips only of #6 scruffy bristle brush into wicker white, and tap up and down along edges of fur. (Test application first on paper to determine desired effect.)

TREE AND STAR

For Santa's gloves and boots, float with licorice, then shade with licorice to deepen the contrast. Highlight boots with tiny strokes of wicker white using the liner brush.

For Santa's belt and buckle, float belt first with burnt umber and then with licorice. Base-paint the buckle

sunny yellow and shade with nutmeg. Highlight the buckle with wicker white.

For Santa's face, first coat with a wash of peach cobbler. Shade with burnt umber. Paint cheeks, nose, and mouth with a float of barnyard red. Paint eyes licorice. Stroke

along right side and bottom edge of each eye with thinned wicker white. Paint brows and add three tiny dot highlights to each eye using wicker white.

For Santa's beard and hair, first shade with country twill. Deepen shading using a float of burnt umber. Use a float of wicker white to highlight hair, mustache, and lower beard.

For bear, first float with nutmeg. Float again using burnt umber. Float barnyard red over inner ears, nose, and cheeks. Shade bow with heartland blue. Dot eyes using stylus dipped in licorice. Add tiny wicker

SANTA AND BEAR

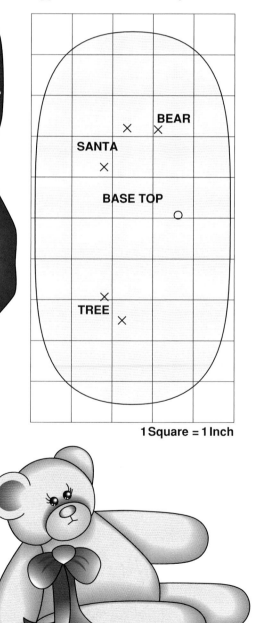

BEAR

SANTA

BASE TOP

TREE

1 Square = 1 Inch

white dot highlights to eyes. Draw eyelashes and mouth with pen.

For candle cup, paint with a wash of barnyard red. Add a few highlights with a wash of sunny yellow. Paint tiny wicker white stars using liner brush.

For base, paint top with two coats of antique gold metallic, and edge and bottom with two coats of licorice. Allow paint to dry and sand lightly between coats.

Speckle painted pieces by dampening toothbrush with water, tapping it to remove excess, and dipping tips into burnt umber. Run a thumb over bristles to blend paint and water. Hold brush approximately 8 inches above each piece and run a thumb over bristles to spatter paint. Rinse brush and repeat procedure using wicker white.

Add tiny dots of gold glitter paint to all stars on candle cup, star, and Santa's clothing. Dot bear's bow and top of each ornament.

Brush all pieces with two coats of varnish, allowing first coat to dry thoroughly before applying second. Hot-glue star to tree top. Place Santa, bear, and tree over Xs on base and hot-glue to position, referring to photo on *page 38.* Drill holes through base and figures at Xs and countersink screw heads. Insert long screws in these holes. Hot-glue candle holder on top of base at O. Drill a hole through base of candle cup and ¼-inch into base, countersinking screw head. Insert short screw in that hole.

KNITTING ABBREVIATIONS	
st st	stockinette stitch
st(s)	stitch; stitches
k	knit
p	purl
lp(s)	loop; loops
sl	slip

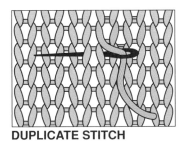
DUPLICATE STITCH

CARDINAL AFGHAN

As shown on page 39, finished afghan measures 54 x 72 inches. Skill Level: for experienced knitter.

MATERIALS
SUPPLIES
Pingouin Fleur De Laine (100-gram or 182-yard skein): 12 skeins of oyster (20); four skeins of wine (07); three skeins of forest green (65); one skein of black (10); and a small amount of yellow (66)
36-inch-long circular knitting needles, sizes 7 and 9, or size to obtain gauge below
Bobbins
Yarn needle
GAUGE:
In stockinette stitch (st st) and color patterns, 25 sts = 6 inches and 23 rows = 4 inches.

INSTRUCTIONS
For beginning border, with smaller needle and green, cast on 227 sts.

Rows 1–9: Knit each row with green.

Rows 10–19: Knit each row with wine.

For holly border, change to larger needle. Work Chart 1, *page 52,* omitting berries. Read chart from right to left for knit rows and from left to right for purl rows. Carry colors not in use loosely along wrong side of afghan. Bring new color from under previous color, twisting to prevent holes.

Row 1 (right side): K 5 wine sts, k 102 oyster sts, place marker, k 13 oyster sts, place a marker, k 102 oyster sts, k 5 wine sts.

Row 2: K 5 wine sts, slipping markers p center 217 sts, k 5 wine sts.

Row 3: K 5 wine sts, follow Chart 1 working in st st; repeat from A to B across to first marker, sl marker, work center 13 sts from Chart, sl marker, repeat C to D across to last 5 sts, k 5 wine sts.

Rows 4–9: Keeping first and last 5 sts in wine garter st, follow chart pattern as established.

Row 10: Removing markers, repeat Row 2.

Row 11: K 5 wine sts, with oyster k 217 sts, k 5 wine sts.

For second border, change to smaller needle and wine.

Rows 1–10: With wine, k 5, p 217, k 5.

Rows 11–20: K 5 wine sts, p 217 green sts, k 5 wine sts.

For afghan body, change to larger needle. K 5 wine sts, p 217 oyster sts, k 5 wine sts.

Row 1: Wind 15 bobbins with wine and 10 with forest green. Keeping 5 sts each edge in wine garter st, work Chart 2 *page 52,* in st st, omitting stitches in black (wings, face, and feet) and yellow (beak). Read chart from right to left for knit rows and from left to right for purl rows. Bring new color from under previous color, twisting to prevent holes. For right side rows, work A to B across, ending last repeat at C.

For right side bobble, with wine, k 1 st; * return this st to left-hand needle; k in front and back of this same st, twice (4 wine lps on right-hand needle); pass second, third, and fourth lp over first lp. Push bobble to right side of fabric *.

For wrong side bobble, with wine, p 1 st; turn, k 1 st; repeat between * s of right side bobble.

Repeat rows 1–94, once; repeat rows 11–94, twice; then work rows 11–82 once, leaving out cardinals in incomplete triangles at top of afghan.

For upper borders, change to smaller needle.

Rows 1–10: K 5 wine, k 217 green, k 5 wine.

Rows 11–20: K 5 wine, k 217 wine, k 5 wine.

Change to larger needle and work rows 1–10 of holly border.

Change to smaller needle and work beginning border, rows 10–19, then work rows 1–9. Bind off all sts in knitting.

Work berries of holly border; wings, face, and feet; and beak in duplicate stitches, referring to diagram, *left.* Weave in ends.

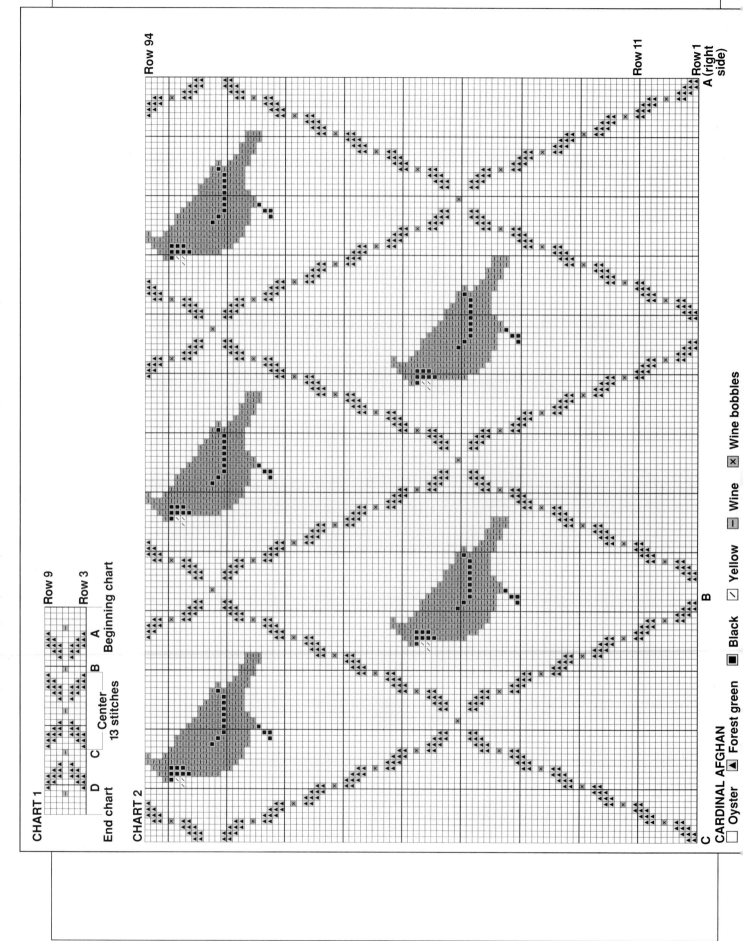

CHART 1

Row 9

Row 3

A
Beginning chart

B

C ⎡ Center
  ⎣ 13 stitches

D

End chart

CHART 2

Row 94

Row 11

A (right side)

Row 1

B

C

CARDINAL AFGHAN

☐ Oyster   ◀ Forest green   ■ Black   ⟋ Yellow   — Wine   ✕ Wine bobbles

SEASHELL CANDLES

*T*his Christmas, enjoy the shells you collected from that favorite sandy beach. Place shells in a tray of sand, carefully leveling them so they'll hold the wax. Spoon melted pink or white candle wax into the shells. (Be sure to follow manufacturer's directions when melting wax.) Insert a wick into the center of each pool of wax, holding it in place until the wax is cool enough to support the wick. Allow to cool completely. Light candles and enjoy the rosy glow.

DESIGNER: BARBARA BARTON SMITH
PHOTOGRAPHER: SCOTT LITTLE

GLISTENING ORNAMENT CANDLE DISH

*T*o create a sparkling and delicate centerpiece, gently arrange small, colorful glass ornaments around a pillar candle in an antique pedestal dish. If you don't have an antique dish, simply use any pretty footed or pedestal dish that will hold the candle and ornaments. In no time at all, you'll have a bright and shining holiday display. For a warm reflected glow, place the dish in front of a mirror.

DESIGNER: ARDITH FIELD
PHOTOGRAPHER: HOPKINS ASSOCIATES

COLONIAL APPLE CANDLEHOLDERS

*O*ur a traditional-looking holiday centerpiece uses real apples as candleholders. Cut a small plug from the top of each apple using an apple corer and insert a small taper candle. Embellish the tops of the apples with orange peel curls and group the candles on a pewter muffin pan or tray. Add a bed of holiday greens for that special Christmas touch.

DESIGNER: ARDITH FIELD
PHOTOGRAPHER: SCOTT LITTLE

CALICO CORN CANDLES

*M*ake Grandma's lovely antique soup tureen the center of attention at your holiday gathering. Fill it with shelled calico popcorn and press votive candles into the corn at different heights. Complete this easy homespun centerpiece by adding a few ears of unshelled corn, a sprinkling of popped popcorn, and sprigs of bright Christmas greenery.

DESIGNER: CAROL FIELD DAHLSTROM
PHOTOGRAPHER: SCOTT LITTLE

CLEVER CANNING JAR CANDLES

*G*ather a few old-time canning jars and fill them with Christmas candies, pretty buttons, colorful marbles, or unpopped popcorn. Position a tea candle in a metal cup atop the contents of each jar. Group several jars together and surround them with fresh holiday greens. Sprinkle the greens with candy and marbles for a glowing, old-fashioned holiday decoration.

DESIGNER: MARGARET SINDELAR
PHOTOGRAPHER: HOPKINS ASSOCIATES

Creative Package Trims

Brighten your holidays with some of our simple-to-make yet festive package toppers. Colorful and bright and created by you, these unique Christmas trims are sure to bring delightful smiles to the ones you love.

BANDANNA BOW

*M*ake Christmas special for a favorite country western fan using two purchased bandannas and matching gift wrap. The ribbons are 1-inch-wide strips torn from one bandanna and wrapped around the gift. For the bow, tear the second bandanna into 1x7-inch strips. Tie the center of the bow fabric strips together with heavy thread, and attach to the package for a casual country package topper.

DESIGNER: BARBARA BARTON SMITH
PHOTOGRAPHER: HOPKINS ASSOCIATES

BUBBLE GUM BOW

*B*uild a bubble gum bow by stacking favorite flavors of bubble gum in three layers and gluing them together with white crafts glue. Glue the bow atop a brightly-colored package, creating a treat for a child of any age.

DESIGNER: MICHAEL DAHLSTROM
PHOTOGRAPHER: HOPKINS ASSOCIATES

SEASHELL COLLECTION TRIM

*W*hether you're celebrating Christmas by the ocean—or recalling vacation memories—this creative shell bow is a delightful accent. Create one by simply grouping shells on a wide pink ribbon and gluing them in place with white crafts glue.

DESIGNER: CAROL FIELD DAHLSTROM
PHOTOGRAPHER: HOPKINS ASSOCIATES

BARRETTE BOW CHRISTMAS TRIM

*B*uy a barrette bow to use as a package topper or create one of your own. To make your own, tie beads onto bright cord and tie the cord into a bow with colorful ribbon. Glue the bow to a French barrette back. Attach the bow to a special gift and create two gifts in one.

DESIGNER: BARBARA BARTON SMITH
PHOTOGRAPHER: HOPKINS ASSOCIATES

GOLD AND SILVER BUTTON BOW

*T*his dazzling button topper is both quick to make and elegantly charming. Shimmering gold and silver buttons found at an antiques shop are grouped into a pleasing arrangement and glued to gold-trimmed ribbon and paper using white crafts glue.

DESIGNER: ARDITH FIELD ● PHOTOGRAPHER: HOPKINS ASSOCIATES

ELEGANT ROSEBUD NECKLACE AND DAINTY BARRETTE TRIMS

*O*ur ribbon trim, *above left*, is really a necklace created by hot-gluing rosebuds to a heart-shaped metal finding and then atop a piece of lace. The rose heart is then hot-glued to a fabric ribbon to complete this elegant choker trim.

For the barrette on the bow, *above right*, simply hot-glue rosebuds to a plain barrette and attach to an ivory bow.

DESIGNER: GAYLE SCHADENDORF ● PHOTOGRAPHER: HOPKINS ASSOCIATES

PINWHEEL BOW

*R*ecall the memories of laughter-filled, sunny days by adding this easy topper to a child's gift. Simply cut the top from a purchased pinwheel and glue it to the package using white crafts glue.

DESIGNER: BARB HICKEY
PHOTOGRAPHER: SCOTT LITTLE

FROM THE TOOL BOX TRIM

*S*ure to please the carpenter in the family, this sparkling bow is created by gluing screws, cup hooks, or any other favorite finding to ribbon wrapped over gold or silver paper.

DESIGNER: MICHAEL DAHLSTROM
PHOTOGRAPHER: HOPKINS ASSOCIATES

SPORTS TICKET BOW

*F*or the sports lover in the family, buy strips of tickets at an office supply store. Trim the gift with ticket ribbon, and then tape 5-inch loops of tickets together to form the bow. Add a favorite baseball card to serve as a gift tag.

DESIGNER: CAROL FIELD DAHLSTROM
PHOTOGRAPHER: HOPKINS ASSOCIATES

On-Call Appetizers

For impromptu entertaining or plan-ahead convenience, try our mouth-watering collection of holiday hors d'oeuvres. Each of these simple but delicious appetizers waits in your refrigerator or freezer until you're almost ready to serve.

PHOTOGRAPHER: HOPKINS ASSOCIATES

in a single layer. Seal, label, and freeze for up to 2 months.

To serve, place the chilled or frozen ribs in a single layer in a shallow baking pan; cover the pan loosely with foil. Heat in a 350° oven about 20 minutes for refrigerated ribs or 45 minutes for frozen ribs or until hot. Transfer ribs to serving platter. Sprinkle with slivered green and red onions, if desired. Makes 12 servings.

PHOTOGRAPHER: SCOTT LITTLE

PASTA-STUFFED TOMATOES

INGREDIENTS
- 3 tablespoons acini di pepe pasta
- ¼ cup firmly packed parsley, finely snipped
- ¼ cup grated Parmesan cheese
- 2 tablespoons crumbled feta cheese (½ ounce)
- 1 tablespoon olive oil or cooking oil
- 1 tablespoon water
- ¼ teaspoon dried basil, crushed
- ⅛ teaspoon garlic powder
- 24 cherry tomatoes
- Alfalfa sprouts (optional)

METHOD
Cook pasta in boiling water for 6 minutes or until tender. Drain well.

Combine parsley, Parmesan, feta, oil, water, basil, and garlic powder. Stir in cooked pasta. Set aside.

Remove stems from tomatoes. Slice a thin layer off the round end of each tomato. Using a grapefruit knife or small spoon, scoop out and discard the pulp, leaving a ¼-inch-thick shell. Invert tomatoes and drain on paper towels. Place tomatoes, stem end down, on a serving plate. Spoon or pipe pasta mixture into tomatoes. Cover; refrigerate for 8 to 24 hours.

To serve, let tomatoes stand at room temperature for 30 minutes. Serve on a bed of alfalfa sprouts, if desired. Makes 24 appetizers.

PHOTOGRAPHER: SCOTT LITTLE

PLUM-GOOD MINI-RIBS

INGREDIENTS
- 3 pounds pork loin back ribs, sawed in half across the bones
- ½ cup red plum jam
- ¼ cup soy sauce
- ¼ cup water
- 3 tablespoons vinegar
- 2 tablespoons cornstarch
- 1 clove garlic, minced
- 2 green onions, finely slivered (optional)
- ⅛ of a red onion, slivered (optional)

METHOD
Cut ribs into single-rib portions. Rinse. Place ribs in a Dutch oven; cover with *water.* Cover and simmer 35 minutes or until ribs are almost tender. Drain ribs and place, meaty side up, in a foil-lined roasting pan.

For sauce, combine jam, soy sauce, water, vinegar, cornstarch, and garlic in a medium saucepan. Cook and stir over medium heat until mixture is thickened and bubbly.

Brush ribs with plum sauce. Bake, uncovered, in a 350° oven for 15 minutes or until ribs are tender and well glazed.

Cool ribs. Place in a covered refrigerator container and refrigerate for 8 to 24 hours. Or, to freeze, arrange cooked ribs in a single layer in a freezer container or wrap in moisture- and vapor-proof wrap

FRUIT AND PROSCIUTTO APPETIZERS

INGREDIENTS
- 2 medium pears
- Lime or lemon juice
- ¼ of a small cantaloupe or honeydew melon
- 3 ounces thinly sliced prosciutto
- Grape clusters
- Quartered orange slices

METHOD
Cut each pear into eight wedges. Brush cut edges with lime or lemon juice. Cut melon into thin wedges. Cut prosciutto into 1-inch-wide strips. Wrap each fruit slice with part of a strip of prosciutto.

Cover and refrigerate for up to 2 hours, if desired. Serve on a platter with grape clusters and orange slices. Makes 8 servings.

PHOTOGRAPHER: HOPKINS ASSOCIATES

encloses the filling, but allows room for filling to expand.

Repeat with remaining phyllo, margarine, and filling to make 36 triangles total. Place triangles on an ungreased baking sheet. Brush with any remaining margarine.

Bake in a 375° oven about 18 minutes or until golden. Serve warm. Makes 36 triangles.

PHOTOGRAPHER: HOPKINS ASSOCIATES

MUSHROOM-CHEESE TRIANGLES

INGREDIENTS

- 1 **cup chopped fresh mushrooms**
- 1 **3-ounce package cream cheese, softened**
- ¼ **cup finely chopped red and/or green sweet pepper**
- 1 **teaspoon white-wine Worcestershire sauce**
- ⅛ **teaspoon garlic powder**
- 12 **sheets frozen phyllo dough (18x14 inches), thawed**
- ⅓ **cup margarine or butter, melted**

METHOD

For filling, in a medium mixing bowl combine the mushrooms, softened cream cheese, sweet pepper, white-wine Worcestershire sauce, and garlic powder.

Unfold phyllo dough. Place one sheet of phyllo dough on a waxed-paper-lined surface. (Cover remaining sheets with damp cloth to prevent drying.) Lightly brush with some of the melted margarine. Place another phyllo sheet on top; brush with some margarine. Cut buttered stack of phyllo lengthwise into six strips.

For each triangle, spoon a *slightly rounded teaspoon* of the filling about 1 inch from one end of each strip. Fold the end over the filling at a 45-degree angle. Continue folding loosely to form a triangle that

SHRIMP PUFFS

INGREDIENTS

- 1 **9½-ounce package frozen miniature patty shells (24)**
- 1 **5- or 6-ounce package frozen, peeled, cooked tiny shrimp, thawed**
- ⅔ **cup dairy sour cream**
- 2 **teaspoons Dijon-style mustard**
- 1 **tablespoon sliced green onion**

Fresh dill

METHOD

Bake patty shells according to package directions; cool completely.

Reserve 24 tiny shrimp; set aside. Chop the remaining shrimp. In a small mixing bowl stir together the chopped shrimp, sour cream, Dijon-style mustard, and green onion until well mixed.

Spoon a scant *1 tablespoon* shrimp mixture into each patty shell. Garnish with reserved tiny shrimp and small sprigs of fresh dill. Serve immediately, or cover and chill for up to 2 hours before serving. Makes 24 servings.

PHOTOGRAPHER: DE GENNARO ASSOCIATES

SAUSAGE AND BROCCOLI SQUARES

INGREDIENTS

- 1 **package refrigerated crescent rolls (8)**
- ⅔ **cup finely chopped, fully cooked smoked turkey sausage (4 ounces)**
- 2 **teaspoons brown mustard**
- ⅔ **cup finely chopped broccoli**
- ⅓ **cup chopped sweet red and/or green pepper**
- ¼ **cup chopped onion**
- ¾ **cup shredded cheddar cheese (3 ounces)**

METHOD

Unroll crescent roll dough. Pat dough onto bottom of a 9x9x2-inch baking pan, overlapping and pressing to fit. Set aside.

Combine the sausage and brown mustard in a small mixing bowl. Spoon evenly over dough in pan. Sprinkle with chopped broccoli, red or green pepper, onion, and cheese. Bake in a 375° oven about 20 minutes or until crust is golden. Cool.

Cut into 25 squares. Layer squares in freezer containers. Seal, label, and freeze for up to 2 months.

To serve, place frozen squares on an ungreased baking sheet. Bake in a 350° oven for 10 to 12 minutes or until heated through. Makes 25.

PHOTOGRAPHER: HOPKINS ASSOCIATES

Festive Holiday Garlands

When the holidays are quickly approaching and time is at a premium, it's still not too late to treat your home to fresh and new decorating ideas. These clever Christmas garlands and personalized tree ideas are a delightfully easy way to brighten your holiday home this season.

COOKIE CUTTER GARLAND

This cheerful garland is a perfect way to say "Merry Christmas" in the kitchen or anywhere in your home. Paint the handles of purchased toy wooden rolling pins red. Drill a hole in one handle of each rolling pin, and using ribbon, tie them to a length of wide black-and-white checked ribbon. Glue ribbon to purchased red cookie cutters and tie to the wide ribbon between the rolling pins, creating some clever holiday fun.

DESIGNER: DONNA CHESNUT ● PHOTOGRAPHER: SCOTT LITTLE

CHRISTMAS BIRTHDAY TREE

*F*or that special birthday at Christmas, why not decorate a tree to celebrate both events? Create our simple birthday garlands and then add bubble gum packs tied with ribbon, colorful blown-up balloons in various sizes, and silly straws for a very unique approach to the season. For a closer look at the garlands and how to create them, see instructions at right.

DESIGNER: DONNA CHESNUT ● PHOTOGRAPHER: SCOTT LITTLE

BALLOON GARLAND

*O*ur festive balloon garland is made by first tying colorful groups of four tiny balloons together using curling ribbon. To finish, just tie the balloon bunches onto a long piece of curling ribbon and drape it among the branches.

JACK AND BALL GARLAND

*T*o make this simple garland, tie jacks along a length of curling ribbon. Attach the ball by tying the ribbon through a center hole made with a drill or ice pick.

DESIGNER: DONNA CHESNUT ● PHOTOGRAPHER: SCOTT LITTLE

ANTIQUE CHRISTMAS CARD GARLAND

*R*ecapture simpler days gone by with this lovely sentimental garland. Tiny plastic clothespins, found at a craft store, hold these charming old Christmas postcards onto country-style cording. What a wonderful reason to spend a winter's day searching through Grandma's old keepsake boxes or the local antiques store!

DESIGNER: DONNA CHESNUT ● PHOTOGRAPHER: SCOTT LITTLE

GARDENER'S BAY LEAF GARLAND

*C*reate a wonderfully fragrant garland from bay leaves, dried apple and orange slices, tiny painted flowerpots, and raffia. Thread bay leaves onto waxed cord, adding fruit slices or a tiny pot every few inches. Add raffia bows at each end, and glue on sprigs of greenery, cinnamon sticks, or even a tiny watering can to complete this natural holiday decoration.

DESIGNER: GERRY BAUMAN
PHOTOGRAPHER: HOPKINS ASSOCIATES

SIMPLE POINSETTIA GARLAND

*O*ur jingling poinsettia garland elegantly frames a snowy scene from the window, or adds traditional grace to a mantel or tree. First, use wire cutters to clip the stamen from the center of nine purchased silk poinsettias. Hot-glue three jingle bells to the center of each, and then hot-glue or wire the poinsettias to a 12-foot-long purchased tapestry cord.

DESIGNER: MARGARET SINDELAR ● PHOTOGRAPHER: HOPKINS ASSOCIATES

GOLFER'S DREAM TREE AND GARLAND

*S*urprise your favorite golfer this year with our golf-lover's garland and tree trims. To make the garland, tie three colorful golf tees in a bunch with gold curling ribbon. Make about 20 tee bunches and tie the bunches evenly spaced to a 2-yard length of gold curling ribbon. Poke holes through six plastic golf balls with an awl. Thread short pieces of ribbon through the holes and tie each to the ribbon strand, spacing them evenly between the tees. After draping the garland through the branches, trim the tree with scorecards, golf pencils, golf gloves, and other favorite golf mementos.

DESIGNER: DONNA CHESNUT ● PHOTOGRAPHER: SCOTT LITTLE

Peace on earth,
and
mercy mild,
God and
sinners
reconciled!
Joyful,
all ye nations,
rise,
Join the
triumph of the
skies;
With th' angelic
host proclaim,
Christ is
born in
Bethlehem!

HARK, THE HERALD
ANGELS SING

Solo or Mixed Voices (use piano n

Hark, the her - ald an - gels sing, "Glo
Christ, by high - est heav'n a - dored; Chr
Hail, the heav'n - ly Prince of peace, Ha

Hark! the herald
angels sing,
Glory to
the new-born King.

Hark, the Herald Angels Sing

"Hark, the herald angels sing, glory to the newborn King." The words of this beautiful Christmas carol set the stage for the glorious angels we have gathered in this holiday collection. Whether they are lovingly painted, carefully stitched, beautifully garnished, or simply sewn, these sweet cherubs are sure to become cherished treasures to adorn your home this Christmas season and for all holiday seasons to come.

PHOTOGRAPHER: HOPKINS ASSOCIATES

Heavenly Angel Trio

Divine young angels, intricately painted on wood, are truly an inspirational accent for your home at Christmastime. Each angel wears a richly painted robe and a crown of dainty pastel flowers. Delicately shaded wings and halos make this grouping a magnificent heirloom collection. Recreate all three for a celestial scene or paint just one to resemble your own little angel. Our color-coded patterns and instructions, beginning on page 78, allow you to paint these glorious pieces with ease.

DESIGNER: SUSAN CORNELISON
PHOTOGRAPHER: HOPKINS
ASSOCIATES

Whimsical Paper Angels

Smiling and granting Christmas wishes, our chubby-cheeked paper angels become cards, ornaments, and an elegant tree topper. Easy to make from watercolor paper and acrylic paints, these projects will be a welcome activity on a winter day. Instructions, including step-by-step photographs, and patterns are on pages 82-86.

DESIGNER: PAT SHAFER
PHOTOGRAPHER: HOPKINS ASSOCIATES

Victorian Cross-Stitched Tree Topper

A special part of Christmas decorating is to be able to enjoy the handmade treasures from years past. Our magnificent cross-stitched angel tree topper, stitched on 28-count linen, is sure to become an heirloom. Begin the tradition by stitching her in time to be the crowning glory for your tree this year. Chart and instructions are on pages 87-89.

DESIGNER: SUSAN CORNELISON ● PHOTOGRAPHER: HOPKINS ASSOCIATES

slightly rounding edges. Wipe off sanding dust with tack cloth.

Coat all sides of each piece with wood sealer, using foam brush. Sand lightly and wipe with tack cloth. Paint all sides with two coats of Queen Anne's lace, allowing paint to dry between coats. Position black transfer paper face down on each wood piece. Place appropriate tracing atop transfer paper, aligning outer edges of design. Tape tracings to wood to prevent slipping. Using a sharp pencil, trace over all lines except those for garment, face, and head wreath detail.

Use the printed color patterns as a guide for painting. Colors on pattern will not exactly match the paint colors, but give a fairly accurate representation.

For each angel's wings, paint wings again using Queen Anne's lace. Add white for highlights. Shade with a mix of AC flesh and fleshtone. Paint outlines and detail using equal parts of pale gold and 14K gold.

For angel one (black-haired angel), mix equal parts sachet pink, white, and Queen Anne's lace and paint outer robe. Blend in additional sachet pink for shading. Paint gown cuffs black cherry. Mix Mendocino red, burgundy rose, and a small amount of sachet pink and paint remainder of gown color. Add additional sachet pink and highlight in vertical streaks across bottom of gown.

Mix burnt umber and brown iron oxide and paint skin. Add a tiny bit of black for shading. Use burnt umber to outline hands. Use Queen Anne's lace to paint halo stripes. Mix equal parts of pale gold and 14K gold; paint remainder of halo. Paint hair using separate dabbing strokes of black and burnt umber, layering colors for depth and definition. When paint is completely

ANGEL THREE

dry, use black transfer paper to transfer face, gown, and head wreath details.

For wreath detail, use dark forest green to paint part of leaves and and wedgwood green for remainder. Paint flowers using a mix of white and sachet pink for edges, a mix of Mendocino red and sachet pink for middle areas, and Mendocino red for centers.

For face detail, use Mendocino red to paint lips. Mix burnt umber and black and use to outline nose, lip midline, and to paint eyebrows. Add AC flesh to burnt umber and highlight area just above eyes. Use white to paint whites of eyes, brown iron oxide for irises, black for pupils, and white for highlights. With black, carefully outline each eye and paint lashes. Use burnt umber to shade inner corner of each eye. Mix a glaze of napthol red light, burgundy rose, and white to blush cheeks.

For gown detail, use Queen Anne's lace to paint wide bands on robe sleeves. Use blue haze to paint half of each leaf and wedgwood green for remaining half. Paint orange flowers using a mix of napthol red light, straw, and Queen Anne's lace; outline using a mix of napthol red light and straw. Paint pink flowers using a mix of Mendocino red and sachet pink; outline with Mendocino red. Mix equal parts of pale gold and 14K gold. Use mixture to dot flower centers and paint all remaining gold detail on gown.

For angel two (blonde angel), use Queen Anne's lace to paint outer robe, using AC flesh to shade and white to highlight. Mix blue haze and midnight blue and paint gown cuffs. Use blue haze to paint remainder of gown. Use Queen Anne's lace and a dry-brush technique to highlight.

Mix AC flesh and fleshtone and paint skin. Add a tiny bit of burnt sienna for shading. Use Queen Anne's lace to highlight fingers and burnt sienna to outline hands. Use Queen Anne's lace to paint halo zigzags; paint remainder using equal parts of pale gold and 14K gold. Use metallic gold to dot halo. Paint hair using separate thin strokes of paint. Use straw, a mix of straw and white, and a mix of straw and burnt sienna. Layer colors for depth and definition, making hair darker around outside and lighter near face. When paint is dry, transfer face, gown, and wreath detail using black transfer paper.

For wreath detail, use green sea to paint part of leaves and dark

forest green for remainder. Paint flowers using white for edges, a mix of white and straw for middle areas, and straw for centers.

For face detail, use a mix of napthol red light and sachet pink to paint lips. Use burgundy rose to paint lip midline. Use burnt sienna to outline nose and paint eyebrows. Use white to paint whites of eyes, blue haze for irises, black for pupils, and white for highlights. Use burnt sienna to outline each eye and paint lashes. Use a mix of AC flesh, fleshtone, and Queen Anne's lace to highlight the nose and the top of each cheek. Use a glaze of napthol red and white to blush cheeks.

For gown detail, use a mix of napthol red light, straw, and white to paint light peach flowers. Use a mix of napthol red light and straw to paint darker peach areas. Use a mix of straw and white to paint yellow flowers and center of large peach flower. Add black centers to yellow flowers. Use blue haze to paint turquoise flowers and leaves, green sea for lighter green leaves, and dark forest green for darker green leaves and dark green flower centers. Use dark forest green to shade lighter leaves. Use Queen Anne's lace to paint lacy detail on gown bodice. Mix equal parts of pale gold and 14K gold and paint tiny flowers. Use green sea to paint leaves. Use gold mixture to paint remainder of gown detail.

For angel three (auburn-haired angel), mix wedgwood green, AC flesh, and white to paint outer robe. Use dark forest green to paint green sleeve bands. Use wedgwood green to outline outer robe. Mix dark forest green and midnight blue and paint gown cuffs. Use dark forest green to paint remainder of gown, allowing paint to streak vertically across bottom.

Paint skin and halo as for blonde angel, omitting dots on halo. Use separate strokes of burnt sienna, straw, and burnt umber to paint hair in same manner as for blonde angel. When paint is dry, transfer

face, gown, and wreath detail using black transfer paper.

For wreath detail, use dark forest green to paint part of leaves and a mix of dark forest green and wedgwood green for remaining leaves. Paint flowers using white mixed with a little napthol red light for edges, an equal mix of napthol red light and white for middle areas, and napthol red light for centers.

For face detail, paint lips, nose, and brows, highlight face, and blush cheeks as for blonde angel. Use burnt sienna to paint lid and lash lines.

For gown detail, use dark forest green to paint green sleeve bands and sachet pink for pink trim. Use equal parts of pale gold and 14K gold to outline pink trim. Use wedgwood green to paint light green leaves; mix in dark forest green for shading as desired. Use tiny, thin strokes of dark forest green to paint dark green leaves. Paint turquoise leaves blue haze. Use a mix of straw, white, and napthol red light for orange accents. Use blue haze to paint turquoise star-shaped flowers; add white to highlight centers and outline each in pink sachet. Use bonnie blue to paint blue flowers; accent with midnight blue and add Queen Anne's lace centers. Paint small pink flowers using white for edges, a mix of sachet pink and white for middle areas, and sachet pink for centers. Paint large pink flowers sachet pink with white and napthol red light accents. Use equal parts of pale gold and 14K for gold centers. Paint all stems with burnt sienna. Paint over stems lightly using equal parts of pale gold and 14K gold. Use the gold mixture to paint remainder of gown detail.

Spray each angel with varnish; allow to dry completely. Rub varnished surfaces lightly with 0000 steel wool; wipe with a tack cloth. Spray pieces with two additional coats of varnish, rubbing with steel wool between coats.

WHIMSICAL PAPER ANGELS

As shown on pages 72–73, angel with bag card measures 7x5 inches; angel and star measures 7x4³⁄₄ inches; tree topper measures 10 inches tall; angel and moon measures 5³⁄₄x4¹⁄₂ inches; singing angel card measures 3³⁄₄x4³⁄₄; and angel with cut wings measures 5³⁄₈x4¹⁄₂ inches.

MATERIALS

Tracing paper; pencil; graphite paper
Watercolor paper and unprinted cards suitable for watercolor
Scherenschnitte scissors
Crafts knife and cutting mat
Small dish of water; waxed paper
#4, 6, and 10 flat artist's brushes
Ivory beige, golden brown, dusty blue, rose, and red acrylic paints
Ultra fine-tip black technical pen
Paper towels; T-pin
2x2-inch piece of poster board or purchased star stencil
Light box or brightly lit window
Masking tape; embossing stylus
Gold glitter paint
Gold glitter paint pen
12 inches of thin gold cord for each ornament

INSTRUCTIONS

Trace desired patterns from pages 83–86 onto tracing paper. Using graphite paper and a pencil, transfer patterns from tracing paper to watercolor paper or unprinted card. For singing angel, position design so fold of card matches fold lines shown on pattern.

Use scherenschnitte scissors or crafts knife and cutting mat to cut around ornament and tree topper designs. Cut out areas indicated inside ornaments and tree topper.

To paint designs, lightly moisten area to be painted. Put a small amount of desired paint color on waxed paper. After side-loading a brush, dip into water and blot lightly on a paper towel. Stroke brush across waxed paper to soften line

PAPER ANGELS

Embossing paper is easy to do and adds an elegant touch to any paper project. Follow these simple step-by-step instructions.

1. An art store will have the supplies and tools for making the paper angels pictured on pages 72-73. You will need a technical pen, embossing stylus, crafts knife, stencils or poster board, and masking tape. Also stock up on acrylic paints and your choice of watercolor paper or unprinted cards.

2. You can use a purchased stencil for embossing or make your own. To make your own stencil, trace one of the small stars, *right,* onto tracing paper. Tape tracing paper onto poster board. Draw around star, leaving an indentation in poster board. Use a crafts knife to cut out star along indented lines.

3. Tape the stencil on a light box or a brightly lit window. Place piece to be embossed, right side down, over stencil. Using stylus, trace outline and center area applying light, even pressure, at least twice.

4. To highlight the embossing, halos, and wings of the angels, lightly paint the area with gold glitter paint. For extra sparkle on the halos, trace them with a gold glitter paint pen.

at edge of paint. While painting, keep colors transparent. When paint is dry, work details using light, quick strokes of pen.

To pierce designs, mark hole placement lightly on right side with a T-pin. Turn design over and place it on cutting mat. Use T-pin to pierce paper at each mark.

To emboss, use purchased stencil or make your own by tracing one of the star outlines from patterns onto tracing paper. Tape tracing paper atop a piece of poster board. Draw around star, leaving an indentation on poster board. Use crafts knife to cut out star along indented lines. Tape stencil on a lightbox or brightly lit window. Place the angel, right side down, over stencil. Using embossing stylus, trace outline and center area at least twice.

For angel with bag card, paint hands, feet, and face ivory beige. Side-load brush with red and paint cheeks using a C-shaped stroke with opening at bottom and heaviest application of paint along top. Side-load brush with golden brown and paint wing, beginning at angel's back and drawing paint out to nearly nothing at edges. Side-load with rose and paint gown, working from darkest areas shown on pattern toward lightest, pulling color out as for wings. For bag, side-load brush with dusty blue and paint as for gown. Work detail using black pen. Emboss stars shown by dotted lines on pattern; paint with glitter paint. Draw halo using glitter paint pen.

For angel and star ornament, paint face, hands, feet, cheeks, and wings as angel with bag. Paint gown in same manner as angel with bag *except,* side-load brush with dusty blue. Paint cuffs, petticoat, and underskirt rose. Work detail using black pen. Brush glitter paint

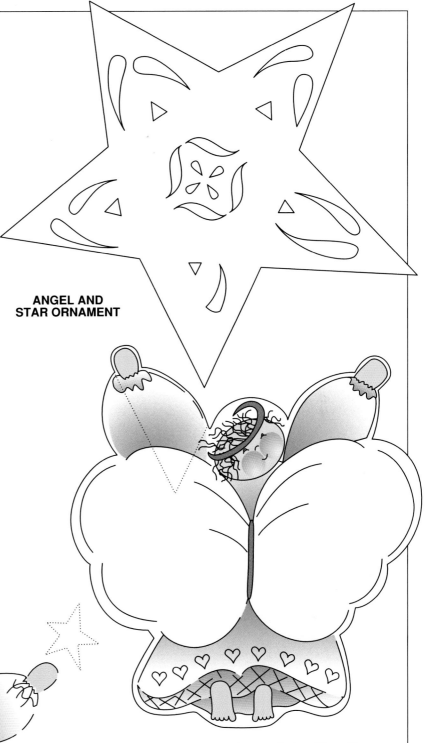

ANGEL AND STAR ORNAMENT

ANGEL WITH BAG CARD

over wings and star. Use glitter paint pen to draw halo and line separating wings. Position angel on star following placement lines on pattern, and glue angel's hands to star. Thread gold cord through top of star and knot ends.

For tree topper, paint face, hands, and cheeks as for angel with bag. Paint hair golden brown. Work detail as for ornaments and cards. Brush glitter paint over halo. Pierce designs on wings and gown.

Emboss star shown by dotted lines on pattern. Gently roll tree topper and overlap straight edges of skirt. Glue or staple edges in place.

For angel and moon ornament, paint and work detail (omitting dots on gown ruffles) as for angel with bag. Pierce holes in gown. Emboss stars indicated by dotted lines on pattern. Brush wings and stars with glitter paint. Paint halo with glitter paint pen. Poke hole in top of moon as shown on pattern. Thread gold cord through hole and knot ends.

For singing angel card, paint as for angel with bag card. Paint mouth red. Work detail using black pen and lightly brush glitter paint onto wings. Draw halo using glitter paint pen.

For angel with cut wings ornament, *page 86,* paint face, hands, and cheeks as for angel with bag. Paint hair golden brown. Work detail, omitting dots. Pierce gown and wings as indicated by dots on pattern. Emboss stars shown by dotted lines on pattern. Draw halo with glitter paint pen. Glue one wing to painted side of angel, following placement line on pattern. Glue other wing to unpainted side, slightly higher than the first. Bend wings outward. Thread gold cord through a wing cutout; knot ends.

Center

ANGEL TREE TOPPER

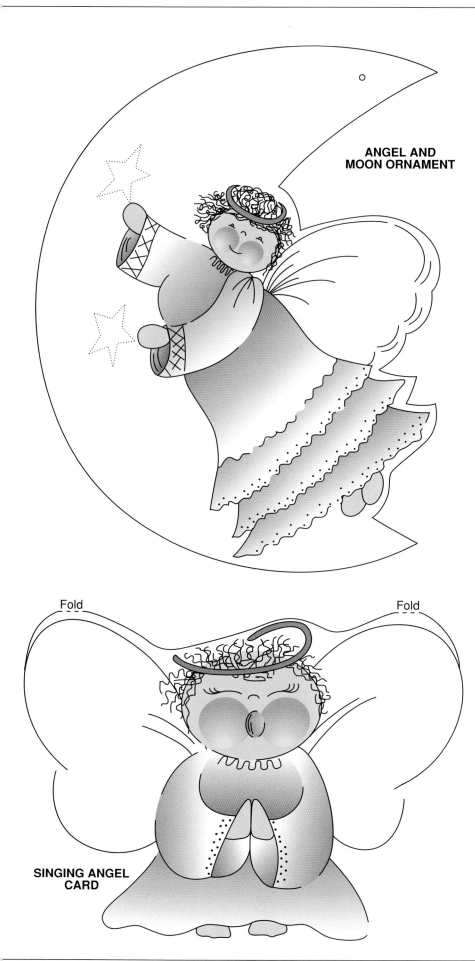

ANGEL AND MOON ORNAMENT

Fold   Fold

SINGING ANGEL CARD

HAPPY SINGING ANGELS

As shown on page 75, angel ornament measures 5 inches tall; large angel measures 26 inches tall.

MATERIALS

For angel ornament

4¼-inch-long piece of 1¼-inch-diameter dowel

4 inches of heavy wire

4x8-inch piece of paper-backed iron-on adhesive

4x8-inch piece of red and green print fabric

8 inches of metallic gold thread

For large angel

Graph paper

9x9-inch piece of 2-inch pine

12x12-inch piece of ¼-inch plywood

24-inch-long piece of 3¼x4-inch landscape timber

One ½-inch-diameter wood button plug

Hot glue gun

Brown wood stain

¾-inch-diameter jingle bell

Poster board or small purchased Christmas tree stencil

Crafts knife and cutting mat

Five 3-inch-long drywall screws

12 inches of heavy wire

Green florist's wire

Natural and red raffia

1x18-inch torn strip of red, green, and white print fabric

1x12-inch torn strip of red and cream mini check fabric

3x4-inch piece of plain brown paper

2¾x3¾-inch piece of white paper

For either angel

Band saw; ¼-inch blade

Sandpaper; stencil brush

Ivory beige, cream, gold, black, red, white, blue, and green acrylic paints

1-inch-wide foam or flat brush

Tracing paper; transfer paper

#1 round and #0 liner brushes

Gold glitter fabric paint

Small sprigs of artificial pepper berries

Drill with 1/16-inch and countersink bits

Curly yellow doll hair; crafts glue

Small sprigs of artificial greenery

**ANGEL WITH CUT WINGS
ORNAMENT**

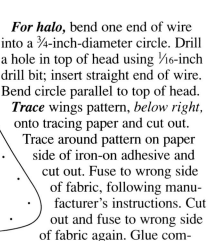

**WINGS
Cut 2**

timber, cut top at 45-degree angle for face. Sand all surfaces smooth.

Paint face, sides and back of face, feet, and wood plug ivory beige. Paint wings and remainder of timber cream. Paint stars gold.

Transfer arm and hand outlines to front of timber, centering hands 5½ inches below edge of face and allowing arm outlines to wrap around sides. Paint hands ivory beige and outlines black.

Use tree pattern, *page 87,* to make a stencil as directed in Step 2 on page 82. Stencil green Christmas trees with gold stars over gown in a random pattern.

Sand edges of face, body, wings, and feet for a worn appearance. Brush gold glitter paint over wings and stars.

Transfer face detail, *right,* onto face. Blush cheeks as directed for ornament. Paint eyelids and pupils black and irises blue. Paint area under iris and the highlights cream. Paint mouth red. Use liner brush to outline eyebrows, eyelashes, and mouth outline black. Glue plug to face for nose. When paint is dry, brush stain over body, face, wings, and feet. Wipe off and allow to dry.

For halo, bend one end of wire into a ¾-inch-diameter circle. Drill a hole in top of head using ¹⁄₁₆-inch drill bit; insert straight end of wire. Bend circle parallel to top of head.

Trace wings pattern, *below right,* onto tracing paper and cut out. Trace around pattern on paper side of iron-on adhesive and cut out. Fuse to wrong side of fabric, following manufacturer's instructions. Cut out and fuse to wrong side of fabric again. Glue completed wings to back of angel. Brush gold glitter paint over gown and wings. Knot ends of metallic thread to make a hanging loop. Glue knotted end to back of head.

Rub short strands of curly hair together to make them frizzy. Glue strands to head top, sides, and back for desired hairstyle.

Glue a few pepper berries to hair. Glue greenery and additional pepper berries to base of hands.

For large angel, enlarge patterns, *page 87,* flopping feet and wings patterns along dashed lines to complete. Cut out feet, wings, and star patterns. Trace around feet pattern once on pine; wings once on plywood; and star four times on plywood. Cut out using band saw. Working from one flat side of

INSTRUCTIONS

For angel ornament, cut one end of dowel at a 45-degree angle for face; sand smooth. Paint face and head areas ivory beige and remainder cream for gown. Trace face, star, and arm detail from patterns, *right.* Transfer face detail to slanted surface, star to center front between face and gown, and arms and hands to gown front. Paint hands ivory beige. Outline hands, arms, and gown neckline in black. Paint eyes, lashes, and brows black. Using liner brush, add a tiny stroke of white along right-hand side edge of each eye, with a tiny stroke of blue beside it. Highlight eyes with dots of white. Paint star and mouth red. Dip stencil brush in red paint, blot until almost dry, and blush cheeks.

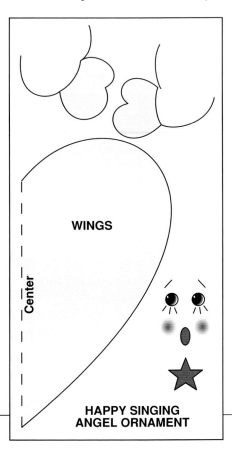

WINGS

Center

**HAPPY SINGING
ANGEL ORNAMENT**

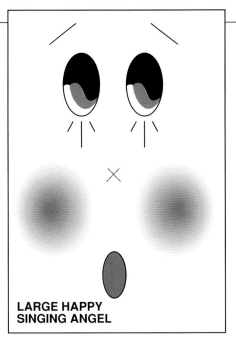

LARGE HAPPY SINGING ANGEL

TREE STENCIL

For halo, bend one end of wire into a circle 2 inches in diameter. Attach as directed for ornament.

Attach hair as directed for ornament *except* use long strands.

Hot-glue wings in place on back of angel and feet to bottom. After gluing, anchor the wings with two drywall screws at center line and the feet with one drywall screw, countersinking screws.

Drill a hole in hand at dot and insert a drywall screw, leaving 1 inch of screw exposed. Drill a hole in each of three stars ½ inch below one point. Attach a piece of florist's wire to each star and the jingle bell, using varying lengths of wire. Secure all four wire ends to screw. Tie a raffia bow onto screw.

Tie red and cream check fabric strip into a bow and glue it to hair. Tie remaining fabric strip around neck, knotting it at back. Glue remaining star to center front.

For book, fold in ¼ inch along all four sides of brown paper rectangle and glue edges in place. Glue white paper rectangle to brown paper, covering glued edges. Fold piece in half to resemble a book. Glue greenery and pepper berries to book front. Glue book to hands above screw.

VICTORIAN TREE TOPPER

As shown on page 74, finished angel is 10½ inches tall.

MATERIALS

FABRICS
14x10-inch piece of 28-count white Cashel linen
14x10-inch piece of polyester fleece
14x10-inch piece of fabric for back
14x10-inch piece white iron-on interfacing

THREADS
Cotton embroidery floss in colors listed in key on pages 88–89
Blending filament in colors listed in key on pages 88–89
Metallic cord in color listed in key on pages 88–89
#8 braid in colors listed in key on pages 88–89

SUPPLIES
Needle; embroidery hoop
Sewing thread
Crafts glue
Erasable fabric marker
1 yard of ⅜-inch-wide gold metallic flat braid
½ yard of ½-inch-wide white flat lace
9x12-inch piece of clear plastic canvas

WINGS Cut 1

Center

FEET Cut 1

Center

ARMS

LARGE HAPPY SINGING ANGEL

1 Square = 1 Inch

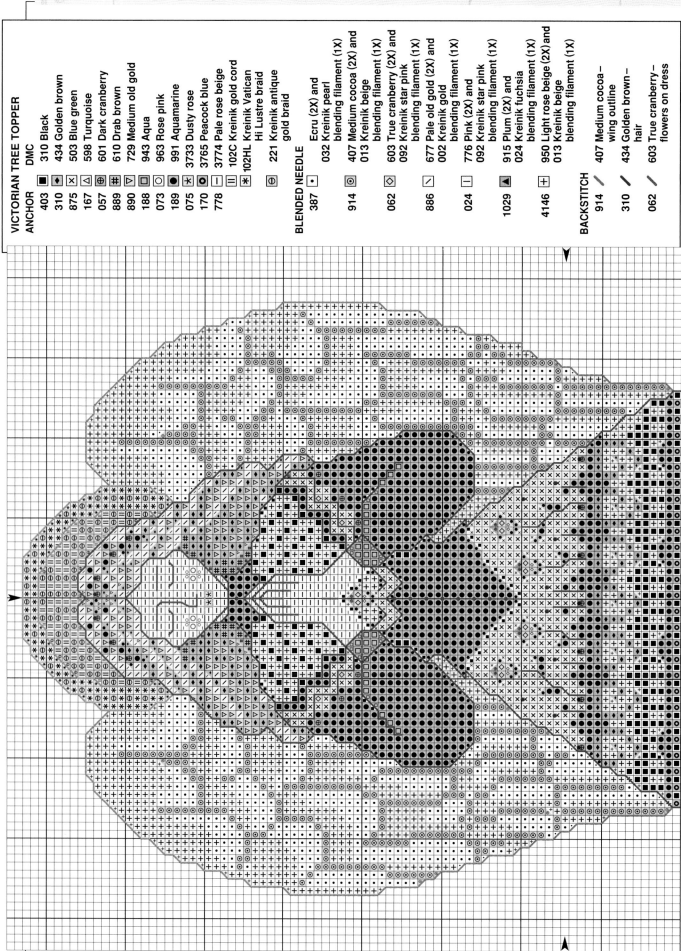

VICTORIAN TREE TOPPER

ANCHOR	DMC	
403	310	Black
310	434	Golden brown
875	503	Blue green
167	598	Turquoise
057	601	Dark cranberry
889	610	Drab brown
890	729	Medium old gold
188	943	Aqua
073	963	Rose pink
189	991	Aquamarine
075	3733	Dusty rose
170	3765	Peacock blue
778	3774	Pale rose beige
	102C	Kreinik gold cord
	102HL	Kreinik Vatican Hi Lustre braid
	221	Kreinik antique gold braid

BLENDED NEEDLE

387	Ecru (2X) and 032 Kreinik pearl blending filament (1X)
914	407 Medium cocoa (2X) and 013 Kreinik beige blending filament (1X)
062	603 True cranberry (2X) and 092 Kreinik star pink blending filament (1X)
886	677 Pale old gold (2X) and 002 Kreinik gold blending filament (1X)
024	776 Pink (2X) and 092 Kreinik star pink blending filament (1X)
1029	915 Plum (2X) and 024 Kreinik fuchsia blending filament (1X)
4146	950 Light rose beige (2X) and 013 Kreinik beige blending filament (1X)

BACKSTITCH

914	407 Medium cocoa – wing outline
310	434 Golden brown – hair
062	603 True cranberry – flowers on dress

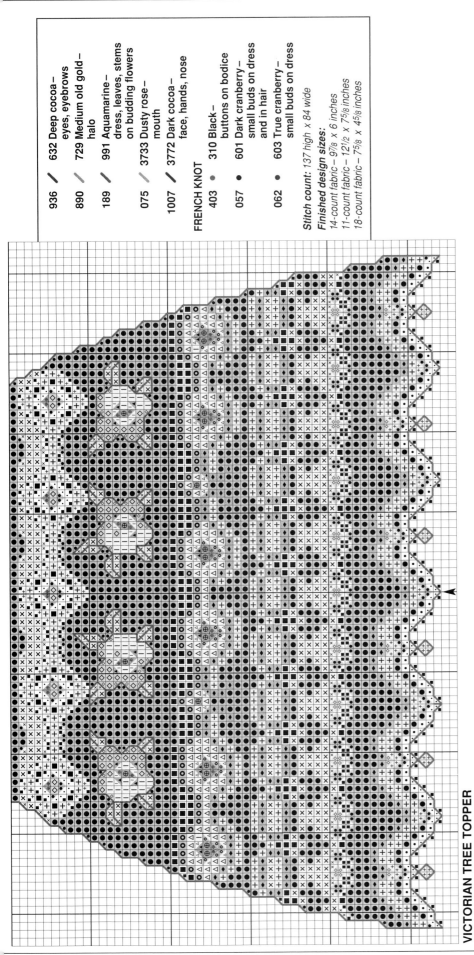

	936	632 Deep cocoa – eyes, eyebrows
	890	729 Medium old gold – halo
	189	991 Aquamarine – dress, leaves, stems on budding flowers
	075	3733 Dusty rose – mouth
	1007	3772 Dark cocoa – face, hands, nose

FRENCH KNOT

	403	310 Black – buttons on bodice
	057	601 Dark cranberry – small buds on dress and in hair
	062	603 True cranberry – small buds on dress

Stitch count: 137 high x 84 wide
Finished design sizes:
14-count fabric – 9⅞ x 6 inches
11-count fabric – 12½ x 7⅝ inches
18-count fabric – 7⅝ x 4⅝ inches

VICTORIAN TREE TOPPER

INSTRUCTIONS

Tape or zigzag edges of fabric to prevent fraying. Find the center of the chart and the center of the fabric. Begin stitching there.

Use three plies of floss, one strand of cord, or one strand of braid to work cross-stitches over two threads of fabric. Work blended needle as specified in key. Work backstitches using one ply. Work French knots using two plies.

Press stitchery from the back. Baste fleece to wrong side, ¼ inch beyond stitching. Following manufacturer's instructions, fuse interfacing to wrong side of back fabric. Sew front to back, right sides facing, along basting line, leaving bottom open. Trim bottom front edge ½ inch beyond cross-stitches and bottom back edge even with front. Trim seam allowances to ¼ inch. Clip curves, turn, and press.

Carefully trace angel's outline onto plastic canvas with marker. Cut out about ⅛ inch inside outline. Insert plastic canvas angel inside fabric angel, pushing it to the front.

Glue gold braid over seam line. Turn bottom edge of fabric up ½ inch and finger press. Hand- or machine-stitch lace to fold.

PLAYFUL CHERUBS

As shown on page 75, finished cherub pin is 2¾x2⅛ inches; finished cherub gift tag is 3x2⅜ inches; and finished cherub ornament is 4¼x4¼ inches.

MATERIALS
FABRIC *for each cherub*
3½x3-inch piece of 14-count ivory perforated paper
THREADS *for each cherub*
Cotton embroidery floss in colors listed in key on page 90
Blending filament in color listed in key on page 90
SUPPLIES *for each cherub*
Needle; scissors
Crafts glue; crafts knife
Paper punch

Continued on page 90

For cherub pin

One ¼-inch-long gold bell

1 inch of ⅛-inch-wide red satin ribbon

3x2½-inch piece *each* of red and green card stock

One 2-inch-long pin back

For cherub gift tag

3x2½-inch piece *each* of red and green card stock

3x4¾-inch piece of ivory card stock

24 inches of thin gold elastic cord

Two small gold heart charms

For cherub ornament

3x2½-inch piece *each* of rose and medium blue card stock

4x4-inch square of tracing paper

4x4-inch piece of ivory card stock

Gold metallic marker

11 inches of ½-inch-wide lace

12 inches of gold cord

Two small gold heart charms

INSTRUCTIONS

Find center of desired chart and center of perforated paper; begin stitching there. Use two plies of floss to work cross-stitches. Work blended needle as specified in key. Work backstiches using one ply of floss. Use floss in color matching skirt to attach bell to center waistline for cherub pin. When stitching is completed, trim one square beyond stitched area as indicated by dotted line on chart.

For cherub pin, knot center of red ribbon around top of gold bell. Center and glue stitched design atop red card stock. Using a pencil, lightly outline shape a scant ⅛ inch beyond cut edge of design. Cut along outline. Next, center and glue design atop green card stock. Outline a scant ⅛ inch beyond red card stock; cut along outline. Glue pin back to back of heart.

For cherub tag, glue stitched design to green and then to red card stock, trimming each as for cherub pin. Fold ivory card stock in half to make a 3x2⅜-inch card. With fold at left, center and glue design atop card. Punch a hole through card in upper left corner. Fold gold cord in half. Loop and knot center of doubled length through hole. Knot ends and tack heart charms to end knot.

For cherub ornament, center and glue design atop rose card stock. Outline shape a scant ⅛ inch beyond cut edge of design and cut out. Fold tracing paper in half. Match folded edge to dotted line on pattern, *below left,* and trace heart pattern; cut out. Trace around tissue pattern onto blue card stock and cut out. Center and glue design atop blue heart. Using gold marker, draw a ⅛-inch-wide border around edge of blue heart. Center and glue blue heart atop ivory card stock. Outline heart shape ³⁄₁₆ inch beyond blue card stock; cut out along outline. Glue lace around outer edge. Punch a hole at top. Loop and knot center of gold cord through hole; knot ends. Tack heart charms to knot.

Note: Each cherub motif may be worked as pin, gift tag, or ornament.

HEART
(for cherub ornament)

Fold

PLAYFUL CHERUBS

ANCHOR		DMC
002	·	000 White
895	○	223 Shell pink
1049	◎	301 Mahogany
403	■	310 Black
9046	◉	321 Christmas red
228	✕	700 Christmas green
293	+	727 Pale topaz
176	△	793 Cornflower blue
4146	−	950 Rose beige
382	▲	3371 Black brown

BLENDED NEEDLE

305	⊞	725 True topaz (1X) and 091 Kreinik star yellow blending filament (1X)

BACKSTITCH

9046	╱	321 Christmas red– mouths
382	╱	3371 Black brown– all remaining stitches

Stitch count: 33 high x 24 wide

Finished design sizes:
14-count fabric – 2⅜ x 1¾ inches
10-count fabric – 3⅜ x 2⅜ inches
6½-count fabric – 5 x 3¾ inches

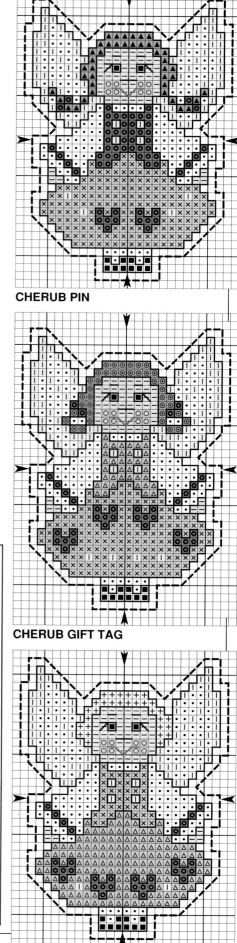

CHERUB PIN

CHERUB GIFT TAG

CHERUB ORNAMENT

O Christmas Tree

"O Christmas Tree, O Christmas Tree, how lovely are thy branches."
For generations, Christmas trees have been the focus of holiday
celebrations. We've shared some wonderful trims for that special
evergreen—from simple ornaments made of paper or popcorn to fancy
crochet trimmings and elegant stars. We even have a festive tree-motif
sweater and an heirloom quilt in a traditional tree pattern.
Share your holiday crafting talents by making the Christmas
tree the center of your holiday decorating.

PHOTOGRAPHER: HOPKINS ASSOCIATES

Country Christmas Ornaments

Leftover buttons from Grandma's button box and scraps of wood and fabric combine to make the irresistible decorations on our charming country Christmas tree. Button Candy Canes *and* Faux Wooden Candles *hang amid painted* Wooden Heart and Star Ornaments. *A calico fabric* Hearts and Stars Garland, *accented with buttons, is draped among the branches, while simple* Manilla Envelope Ornaments *hold sweet surprises. A* Button Star Topper *crowns our holiday tree. Instructions and patterns for all these decorations and the* Popcorn Stars *shown on the cover begin on page 99.*

DESIGNERS: FABRIC GARLAND, KATHY MOENKHAUS;
ALL OTHER DESIGNS, DONNA CHESTNUT AND CAROL DAHLSTROM
PHOTOGRAPHERS: TREE, HOPKINS ASSOCIATES; ALL OTHER
photographs, SCOTT LITTLE

Folk Art Trims

*W**ork Christmas magic with plain papier mâché ornaments and acrylic paint.
Simple shapes are transformed into imaginative works of art by applying paint in
bright colors and geometric patterns. Instructions are on page 101. To complement
these vivid trims, personalize purchased cookie cutters with paint pens.*

DESIGNER: DIANE SHANNON ● PHOTOGRAPHER: SCOTT LITTLE

Elegant Marbleized Star Ornaments

*A stellar accent for your holiday displays, our marbleized paper stars are a project
the whole family will enjoy. Even your little one can help swirl paint atop liquid starch
to help make the magnificent marbled designs. Step-by-step photographs are on page
102. After the paint has dried on the paper, follow our folding and cutting diagrams
on page 103 to complete four, five, or six-pointed stars.*

DESIGNER: SUZANNE YELKIN • PHOTOGRAPHER: HOPKINS ASSOCIATES

Charming Tree Sweater

Celebrate the holidays and spread good cheer wearing this well-loved symbol of the Christmas season. It only takes an afternoon to create this special sweater—a fabric tree is simply appliquéd to a purchased sweater and trimmed with Christmas button ornaments, charms, and gold braid garland. Instructions and pattern are on pages 104–105.

DESIGNER: MARGARET SINDELAR
PHOTOGRAPHER: HOPKINS
ASSOCIATES

Fabric Tree Boxes

Here's a very special way to present a gift. Purchased tree-shaped boxes take on a whole new look when covered with holiday fabrics and sparkling trims. Use them to share homemade goodies or as a substitute for traditional gift wraps. The instructions on page 104 can be adapted to almost any shape box.

DESIGNER: MARGARET SINDELAR
PHOTOGRAPHER: HOPKINS ASSOCIATES

Pine Tree Quilt

Stitched with love, our Pine Tree Quilt *will protect your family from those winter chills well beyond the Christmas season. Cleverly arranged pieces resemble pine trees topped with star-shaped buttons. The trees are combined with striking blocks of red fabric in a pinwheel configuration. This snuggly blanket is machine quilted so you can sleep under it this Christmas Eve! Instructions and patterns are on page 106–107.*

DESIGNER: MARGARET SINDELAR ● PHOTOGRAPHER: SCOTT LITTLE

Lacy Crocheted Snowflakes

Try imitating Mother Nature by creating these delicate and lacy snowflakes. Crocheted from metallic thread, the snowflakes have a sparkling and dainty beauty that will remind you of the very loveliest of quiet snowy days. Instructions for all six of these exquisite ornaments begin on page 107.

DESIGNER: MELODY MACDUFFEY ● PHOTOGRAPHER: HOPKINS ASSOCIATES

HEARTS AND STARS GARLAND

As shown on pages 92–93 and cover, finished garland measures approximately 2⅔ yards long.

MATERIALS

8x10-inch piece of template plastic
⅛ yard *each* of three 45-inch-wide red calicos
⅛ yard *each* of three 45-inch-wide gold calicos
⅛ yard *each* of three 45-inch-wide blue calicos
⅛ yard of 45-inch-wide green calico
Erasable fabric marker
⅛ yard of paper-backed iron-on adhesive
⅛ yard of fleece; fabric glue
Red, blue, green, and gold cotton embroidery floss
5½ yards of ecru carpet thread
Assorted buttons
Tapestry and sewing needles

INSTRUCTIONS

For ornaments, trace pattern outlines, *right,* onto template plastic. Draw a freehand line around perimeter of each, adding ⅜ to ⅝ inch all around. Cut out shapes along second outlines. Draw around templates onto fabrics, making six pairs of each of the four shapes on a variety of fabrics; cut out. From fleece, cut six of each shape.

Trim templates to original outlines and trace around these smaller templates on paper side of iron-on adhesive, making twelve of each shape. Fuse two of each shape to each of six fabrics. Cut out. From remaining fabric, tear fourteen ¾x4-inch strips.

Following manfacturer's instructions, fuse smaller hearts onto larger hearts; smaller stars onto larger stars of same shape. Make two of each color and print combination, so when sewn together, fronts and backs match.

Use one ply of floss in desired color to work straight stitches around edge of smaller shapes as shown on diagram, *above right.*

Layer appropriate fleece shape between each matching pair of fabric shapes. Use one ply of floss to work a running stitch around perimeter ⅛ inch from edge, referring to diagram, *below.* Glue button to center of each side.

For garland, tie a small loop in one end of carpet thread. Thread other end into tapestry needle. Thread a button onto needle, push it to the loop, and secure with a half knot. Thread on three more buttons and half knot each in place 1 to 1½ inches apart. Thread an ornament, pushing needle through

center ¼ inch from top, Secure with a half knot 1½ inches from last button. Continue threading four buttons and an ornament onto thread until all have been used.

Tie a fabric strip around thread between second and third buttons between each shape.

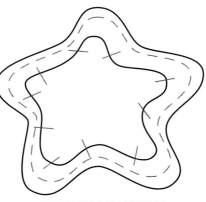

STITCHING EXAMPLE

WOODEN HEART AND STAR ORNAMENTS

As shown on pages 92–93 and cover.

MATERIALS *for one of each*

Drawing paper; pencil
10x14-inch piece of ¼-inch plywood
12x16-inch piece of ½-inch pine
Red, gold, and blue acrylic paint
½- and 1-inch-wide flat paintbrushes
Five assorted buttons
Five 24x½-inch torn strips of red and blue plaid fabrics
Hot glue gun
Medium grit sandpaper
Drill and ⅛-inch drill bit
Bandsaw

HEARTS AND STARS GARLAND AND WOODEN ORNAMENTS

INSTRUCTIONS

Use patterns, *page 99*, as a guide to draw a 2¾x2⅞-inch small star, 4⅜x3¾-inch large star, 4⅜x2¾-inch narrow heart, and 6¾x4¼-inch wide heart pattern. Or, use commercial copier to enlarge patterns on page 99 to approximate sizes. Cut out patterns. Draw around each pattern onto ½-inch pine.

Cut the patterns freehand, trimming ¼ to 1 inch from each; trace on ¼-inch plywood. Cut out all pieces using the bandsaw. Sand edges lightly.

Paint shapes, using contrasting colors on pieces with same shape. When paint is dry, sand all edges once more for a worn look.

Glue plywood shapes atop pine. Hot glue a button to center front of each ornament. Drill a ⅛-inch hole through each ornament near top. Thread a fabric strip through hole; tie ends to make a hanging loop.

BUTTON STAR TOPPER

As shown on page 93 and cover.

MATERIALS

Drawing paper
Pencil
12x18-inch piece of ¼-inch plywood
Red and gold acrylic paint
Small flat paintbrush
140 to 150 assorted buttons
36 inches of 18-gauge wire
Hot glue gun
Medium-grit sandpaper
Drill and ⅛-inch drill bit
Bandsaw

INSTRUCTIONS

Use the large star pattern, *page 99*, as a guide to draw a 10½x9-inch star pattern. Or, use a commercial copier to enlarge the pattern to approximate size. Cut out and draw around the pattern on the plywood. Cutting the pattern freehand, trim 1 to 1¼ inches from the edges and draw around the pattern on the plywood again. Cut out both stars using the bandsaw. Sand all edges lightly with sandpaper.

Paint large star red and small star gold. Sand edges for a worn look. Glue small star atop large star.

Drill two holes, ½ inch apart, about 4½ inches from top point of star. Cut wire length in half and thread both pieces through holes with ends extending out back (for securing ornament to tree).

Glue buttons to front of small star in a random overlapping pattern.

FAUX WOODEN CANDLES

As shown on pages 92-93 and cover, each candle is 4 inches tall.

MATERIALS

For each candle
4-inch-long piece of ⁵⁄₁₆-inch-diameter dowel
Pencil sharpener (optional)
Drill and ³⁄₃₂-inch drill bit
Acrylic paint in desired color
½-inch flat paintbrush
Medium grit sandpaper; crafts glue
Four 1-inch-long pieces of string
Tree clip-on candleholder

INSTRUCTIONS

Sharpen one end of dowel with a pencil sharpener, if desired, leaving a ⅛-inch-diameter flat surface at tip. (Or, leave top of dowel flat to give the appearance of a candle that has been burned.)

Drill a ³⁄₃₂-inch hole in top of dowel. Paint dowel; allow it to dry. Sand lightly for a worn look. Glue ends of string pieces into hole. Place finished candle in candleholder.

MANILLA ENVELOPE ORNAMENTS

As shown in a variety of sizes on page 93 and cover.

MATERIALS

Small manilla clasp envelopes
Paper punch; thin twine
Assorted plastic buttons
Colorful gift wrap, shredded ribbon, and candy

INSTRUCTIONS

Cut the flap off the envelope, if desired. On the side of the envelope that is (or would be) under the flap, punch a small hole near each corner, ¼ inch from the top edge. Cut three pieces of twine, each about the length of the envelope. Tie one end of one piece of twine through each hole. Tie two buttons onto each strand of twine, spacing the buttons at random. Tie the ends of the twine strands together in a knot.

Punch two more holes, close together, in the back of the envelope near the top center and thread remaining piece of twine through hole. Knot ends together to make a hanging loop. Fill bag as desired.

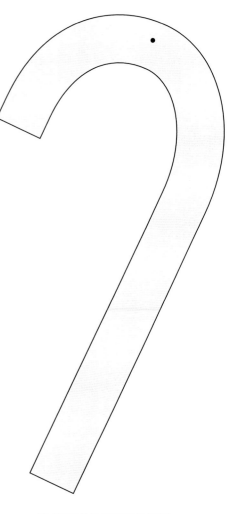

BUTTON CANDY CANE

BUTTON CANDY CANES

As shown on pages 92–93 and cover, candy cane is 5 inches long.

MATERIALS

For each ornament

4x6½-inch piece of ¼-inch plywood
Red acrylic paint; small paintbrush
Eight ⅝-inch red buttons
Eight ⅝-inch cream buttons
10-inch-long piece of monofilament
Hot glue gun
Medium grit sandpaper; tracing paper
Drill and ⅛-inch drill bit; bandsaw

INSTRUCTIONS

Trace pattern, *left*, onto tracing paper and cut out. Draw around pattern on plywood and cut out using bandsaw. Drill a hole through top at dot.

Sand cutout lightly and paint red. Sand edges once more for a worn look. Thread monofilament through hole and knot ends to make a hanging loop. Glue buttons to candy cane front, alternating colors and overlapping edges.

POPCORN STARS

Make extra stars, popcorn balls, or other shapes for a holiday snack, except omit hot-glued trimmings shown on cover.

INGREDIENTS

**18 cups popped popcorn (about
    1 cup unpopped)**
2   cups sugar
1½ cups water
½   cup light corn syrup
1   teaspoon vinegar
½   teaspoon salt
1   teaspoon vanilla
**3- to 4-inch-diameter star-shaped
    gelatin molds**
Round wrapped peppermints
For nonedible ornaments
    Purchased tassels; rattail cord
    Hot glue gun; plaid ribbon

METHOD

Remove unpopped kernels from popped corn. Place popcorn in a greased 17x12x2-inch baking pan. Keep warm in a 300° oven while preparing syrup.

Butter sides of a heavy 2-quart saucepan. In saucepan combine sugar, water, corn syrup, vinegar, and salt. Cook over medium-high heat until boiling, stirring constantly with a wooden spoon to dissolve sugar. (Avoid splashing mixture on sides of pan.) Cook over medium heat, stirring occasionally, to 250° (hard ball stage).

Remove from heat and stir in vanilla. Pour syrup over popcorn and stir gently to coat. Cool until popcorn can be handled easily. Use buttered hands to press popcorn into greased molds. Unmold and press a mint into center of each.

For nonedible ornaments, hot-glue a tassel between two points of each star. Fold a 6-inch piece of rattail cord in half. Hot-glue ends of cord to point of star opposite tassel. Tie ribbon in a bow around cord.

FOLK ART TRIMS

As shown on page 94, heart ornaments measure 2¾ inches across; balls measure 2½ and 3 inches in diameter.

MATERIALS

**Purchased papier mâché ornaments:
    puffy hearts, 2½-inch-diameter
    balls, and 3-inch-diameter balls**
White acrylic primer
Acrylic paints in desired colors
Gold metallic pen; artist's brushes
Gloss interior wood finish
Paper grocery sack; pencil

INSTRUCTIONS

Paint all ornaments with one coat of primer and allow to dry. Rub primed surfaces with a piece of grocery sack to remove any bumps raised by primer. Referring to photograph on page 94, draw desired pattern on each ornament, using combinations of stripes, zigzags, squiggles, stars, and hearts. Add tiny dots by dipping handle of flat brush into paint and touching it to ornament surface. Draw gold lines using gold metallic pen. Allow paint to dry.

Brush varnish over one-half of each ornament at a time, allowing twenty minutes drying time before varnishing other half. Apply a second coat in same manner. Let completed ornaments dry overnight.

MARBLEIZED STAR ORNAMENTS

As shown on page 95, stars measure from 2 to 8½ inches across, depending on size of paper used to create star.

MATERIALS

Plastic table covering or newspapers
**Two large rectangular baking dishes
    or plastic dishpans**
Liquid laundry starch
Custard cups or small containers
Acrylic paint in desired colors
Artist's brushes; white bond paper
Marbleizing tools (see page 102)
Newspaper strips; gold metallic paint

INSTRUCTIONS

To marbleize paper, cover work surface with plastic covering or newspapers. Pour starch into one baking dish to a depth of 2 inches. Fill remaining dish with cool water.

In custard cups, dilute each paint color until it just barely drips from a brush. Gently allow paint to drop from ends of brushes onto surface of starch until the surface of the starch is nearly covered.

Create a pattern in the paint. Drag a comb, made by inserting plastic picks into a block of plastic foam, or similar tool through the paint for a pattern of wavy lines.

For an arched pattern, comb paint in one direction and then in the perpendicular direction. *For a pebble pattern,* leave paint drops as they are. *For a feather pattern,* use ice pick to make parallel lines back and forth through paint, alternating direction. *For a star burst pattern,*
Continued on page 103

STEP-BY-STEP MARBLEIZING

You'll find lots of uses for marbelized paper during the holiday season. It makes beautiful paper ornaments like the folded stars on page 95. Dip larger sheets for gift wrap or try heavier paper for Christmas cards.

PHOTOGRAPHER: HOPKINS ASSOCIATES

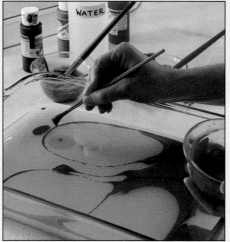

1. You probably already have most of the supplies you need to make beautiful marbleized paper. Gather a large bottle of liquid starch, several colors of acrylic paints, two large flat baking dishes or dishpans, a few custard cups, small bowls, or empty margarine containers, and paint brushes, plus a variety of tools to create patterns in the paint.

2. Fill one baking dish or dishpan with starch to a depth of 2 inches; fill the second one with cool water. In custard cups or other small containers, dilute each paint color until it just barely drips from a brush. Then drip colors on top of the starch until the surface is nearly covered.

3. Create a pattern in the starch using one of the methods on page 101, or experiment with a feather, nut pick, ice pick, coiled rubber cord, wire whisk, fork, or wide-toothed hair comb. Move the desired tool through the paint in straight lines, at geometric angles, in circles, or in rays. Even if you leave the dots undisturbed, no two patterns will be the same.

4. Hold a piece of paper by opposite corners and bend it gently so the paper sags slightly. Lay it gently on top of the paint, but do not allow the paper to sink below the surface. Immediately lift paper back out of the starch. Hold it over the dish and allow the paint to drip off for 10 seconds.

5. Rinse paper in the dish of plain water. Lift paper out of water and allow it to drip for about 15 seconds or until most of the water has dripped off. Lay the paper, paint side up, flat on a paper towel-covered work surface to dry.

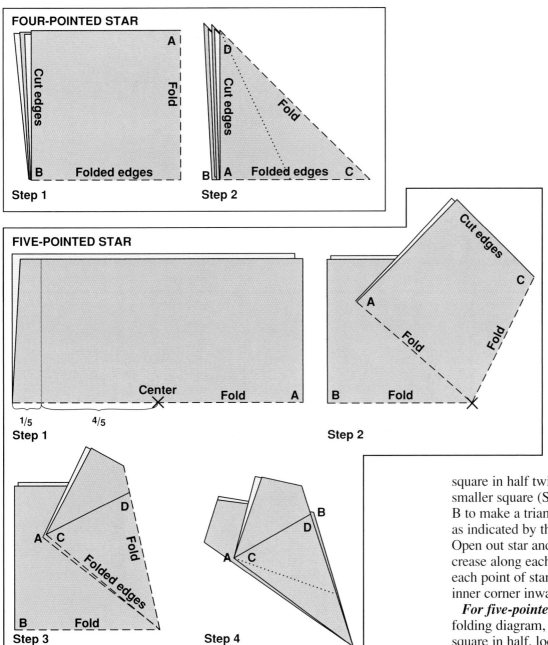

FOUR-POINTED STAR

Step 1

Cut edges · Fold · Folded edges · A · B

Step 2

Cut edges · Fold · Folded edges · D · A · B · C

FIVE-POINTED STAR

Step 1

Center · Fold · A · 1/5 · 4/5

Step 2

Cut edges · Fold · Fold · A · B · Fold

Step 3

Fold · Folded edges · A · C · D · B · Fold

Step 4

A · C · D · B

use ice pick to gently pull points of paint outward from round drops. *For a swirl pattern,* swirl ice pick in a circular motion through paint.

Hold piece of paper to be marbleized by opposite corners and bend it lightly so it sags slightly in the center. Lay it gently atop paint, but do not allow it to sink below the surface. Immediately lift paper back out of starch. Holding paper over tub, allow it to drip for about 10 seconds.

Rinse paper in water dish. Lift paper out of water and allow it to drip for about 15 seconds. When most of water has dripped off, lay it flat on a paper-towel-covered work surface to dry.

Add additional paint for next paper, if desired. To remove paint from starch before adding new colors, skim with newspaper strips.

For each star, when paper is completely dry, smooth it by ironing on the wrong side. (Cover ironing board with a protective cloth.) Cut paper into squares.

For four-pointed star, refer to folding diagram, *above.* Fold

square in half twice to make a smaller square (Step 1). Fold A to B to make a triangle (Step 2). Cut as indicated by the dotted line. Open out star and make a sharp crease along each fold, creasing each point of star outward and each inner corner inward.

For five-pointed star, refer to folding diagram, *left.* After folding square in half, locate center of folded edge and an imaginary line four-fifths of distance from center of folded edge to left edge (Step 1). Fold A to imaginary line, using center of folded edge as pivot point (Step 2). Next, fold C to A (Step 3). Fold B around back to meet opposite point D (Step 4) and cut as indicated by dotted line. Open out star and crease points and inner corners as for four-pointed star.

For six-pointed star, refer to folding diagram, *page 104.* After folding square in half, locate center of folded edge (Step 1). Fold piece into thirds, using center of folded edge as bottom point (Step 2).

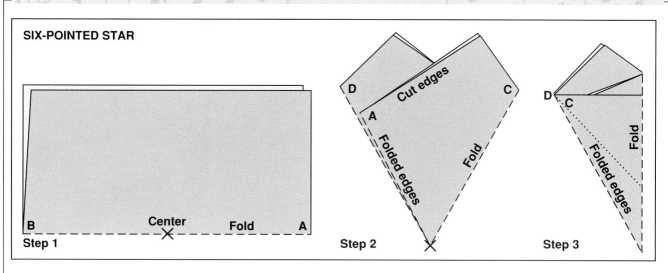

SIX-POINTED STAR

Step 1 · B · Center · Fold · A

Step 2 · D · Cut edges · C · A · Folded edges · Fold

Step 3 · D · C · Folded edges · Fold

Next, fold resulting shape in half, matching C to D, and cut as indicated by dotted line (Step 3). Open out; crease points and inner corners as for four-pointed star.

Paint a metallic gold border along edges of each star.

FABRIC TREE BOXES

As shown on page 96, small box is 9x7½x3 inches; medium box is 11x9x3½ inches; and large box is 13x10¼x4 inches.

MATERIALS

For small box

Purchased 9x7½x3-inch papier mâché tree-shaped box
⅓ yard of 45-inch-wide red Christmas print fabric
9x8-inch piece of green felt
⅞ yard of gold metallic flat trim

For medium box

Purchased 11x9x3½-inch papier mâché tree box
½ yard of 45-inch-wide green Christmas print fabric
11x9-inch piece of green felt
1⅛ yard of red flat trim
1 yard of ⅞-inch-wide gold-edged red ribbon

For large box

Purchased 13x10¼x4-inch papier mâché tree box
⅝ yard of 45-inch-wide red Christmas print fabric
13x10-inch piece of red felt
1¼ yards of red flat braid
1¼ yards of gold metallic lace trim

For each box

⅓ yard of 16-inch-wide paper-backed iron-on adhesive
9x12-inch piece of fleece
Gold charms, jingle bell charms, and/or acrylic stones
Crafts glue
Measuring tape
Yardstick

INSTRUCTIONS

For each box, trace around the lid top twice onto fleece and once onto paper side of iron-on adhesive. Cut out the fleece and iron-on adhesive shapes. Glue one fleece shape to the lid and glue remaining piece atop first. Fuse iron-adhesive tree shape to the back of Christmas print. Cut out 1 inch beyond adhesive. Following manfacturer's instructions, fuse fabric to the fleece on lid. Clip every inch around fabric extending beyond the top edge and glue it to sides of lid.

Measure perimeter of lid and cut a 2-inch-wide strip of fabric the same length as the perimeter measurement. Glue the strip around edge of the lid. Clip extra width of strip every inch, turn it to inside of lid, and glue.

Measure the box bottom depth and perimeter. Cut a strip with these dimensions from the fabric. Glue the strip around sides of box bottom. Trace box bottom onto felt. Cut out felt and glue it to the bottom of the box.

For small box, glue gold trim to lid around top edge. For medium box, glue red braid to lid as on small box. For large box, glue gold lace around lid top edge. Glue red braid atop lace. Glue the charms, bells, and/or acrylic stones to the top in desired pattern.

CHARMING TREE SWEATER

As shown on page 96, tree design is 8¼x7½ inches.

MATERIALS

Graph paper
Pencil
9x8½-inch piece of paper-backed iron-on adhesive
9x8½-inch piece of green print fabric
Long sleeved light green cotton mock turtleneck sweater
½ yard of ⅜-inch-wide metallic gold trim
⅛-inch-wide gold metallic ribbon (Kreinik 002)
Tapestry needle
Thread to match fabric
Nineteen novelty Christmas buttons
Twelve red jingle bell charms
Fabric glue

INSTRUCTIONS

Trace the pattern, *right,* and cut out. Trace around the pattern on the paper side of the iron-on adhesive; cut out and fuse to the wrong side of the green print fabric following manufacturer's instructions. Cut out fabric tree.

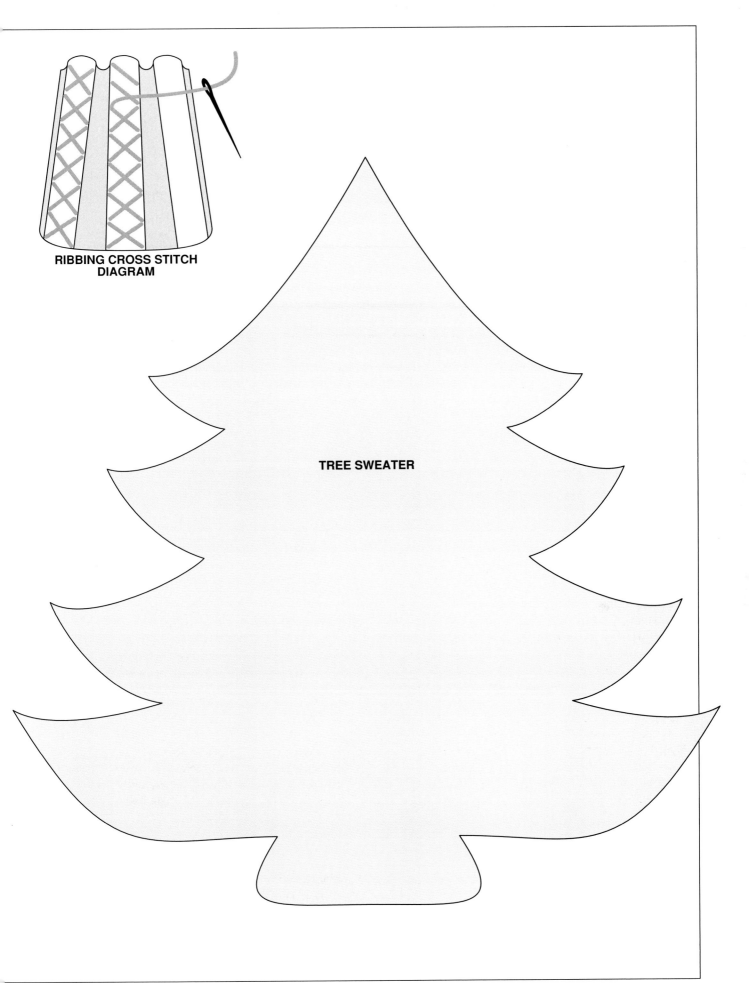

RIBBING CROSS STITCH DIAGRAM

TREE SWEATER

Remove the paper backing from the adhesive and center the top point of the tree 1½ inches below the base of the neck ribbing. Following manufacturer's instructions, fuse the tree to the sweater. Machine-satin-stitch around the perimeter of the tree.

Glue gold trim to the tree in a zigzag pattern to resemble garland, referring to photograph, *page 96.* Sew buttons and bells in a random pattern to resemble ornaments on the tree.

Use ⅛-inch-wide gold ribbon and tapestry needle to work nine cross-stitches down each rib around the neck, referring to diagram, *page 105.* In same manner, work eleven cross-stitches down each rib of the cuffs.

PINE TREE QUILT

As shown on page 97, quilt measures 60x60 inches.

MATERIALS
Tracing paper; pencil
Cardboard or plastic for templates
1½ yards of 45-inch-wide white-on-white print cotton fabric
1½ yards of 45-inch-wide green print cotton fabric
⅓ yard of 45-inch-wide brown print cotton fabric
3¾ yards of 45-inch-wide red print cotton fabric
60x60-inch piece of fabric for quilt back
White and red sewing threads
60x60-inch piece of quilt batting
Thirty-six 1⅛-inch gold star buttons

INSTRUCTIONS
Preshrink, dry, and press all fabrics before cutting pieces.

Trace pattern pieces A, B, C, and D, *below,* onto tracing paper and cut out. Draw around each piece onto cardboard or plastic and cut out to make templates. Label templates and mark each with an arrow indicating fabric grain direction. All patterns and measurements include ¼-inch seam allowances.

From white fabric, cut 216 B triangles and 72 D rectangles. From the green fabric, cut 108 A triangles and four 2x54-inch inner border strips. From the brown fabric, cut 36 C rectangles. From the red fabric, cut thirty-six 4½x8½-inch rectangles and four 4½x64-inch outer border strips.

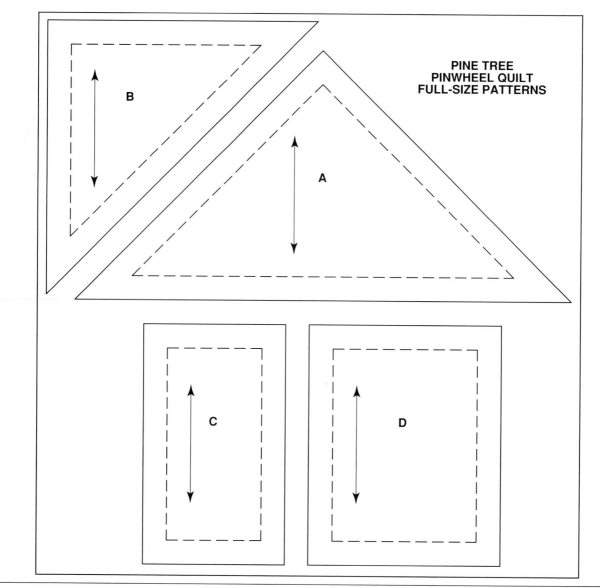

PINE TREE
PINWHEEL QUILT
FULL-SIZE PATTERNS

B

A

C

D

Make each quarter-block first. To make one quarter-block, refer to Figure 1, *below.* Sew long side of a B triangle to each short side of an A triangle. Make three green and white BAB rectangles. Next, join one long side of a D rectangle to each long side of one C rectangle. Referring to Figure 1 for color position, join three green and white rectangles to form a strip. Sew one long side of brown and white DCD rectangle to green end of strip.

Turn the patchwork strip so the tree design is right side up and mark the right-hand side. Sew one long side of a red rectangle to marked side of strip to complete quarter-block.

To make one quilt block, piece four quarter-blocks into a block, referring to Figure 2 for placement. Make nine blocks.

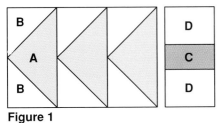

Figure 1

To assemble quilt top, join three blocks in a horizontal row. Repeat twice to make three rows. Join rows horizontally to make a square with three rows of three blocks each.

Sew a green inner border strip to each side of the quilt, mitering corners. In same manner, sew a red outer border strip to each side of the quilt.

Layer the quilt top, the batting, and the back. Working from the center of the quilt outward in a spoke pattern, baste the layers together. Machine-quilt on seam line around each quarter-block and each side of the green border.

From remaining red fabric, cut approximately seven yards of 2½-inch-wide binding. Fold the binding in half, wrong sides together, so it is 1¼ inches wide and press. Matching raw edges, sew the binding to the front of the quilt. Trim any excess batting and back fabric to ¼ inch. Turn the folded edge of the binding to the quilt back and slip-stitch it in place.

Hand-sew one star button to the top of each tree.

Figure 2

CROCHET ABBREVIATIONS	
ch	chain
dc	double crochet
hdc	half double crochet
lp	loop
rep	repeat
rnd	round
sc	single crochet
sk	skip
sl st	slip stitch
sp	space
st(s)	stitch(es)
tr	triple crochet

LACY CROCHETED SNOWFLAKES

As shown on page 98, finished snowflakes measure 3½ to 4¼ inches in diameter.

MATERIALS
2 spools of DMC gold metallic embroidery thread
2 spools DMC silver metallic embroidery thread
"B" aluminum crochet hook
Fabric stiffener; small paint brush

INSTRUCTIONS
Use a double strand of thread throughout. Picot = ch 3, sl st in previous st.

#1

For #1 gold snowflake, chain 6, join with sl st to form ring.

Rnd 1: Ch 3, 15 dc in ring, end with sl st in 3rd ch of beg ch-3.

Rnd 2: (Ch 3, picot, ch 3, sk 2 dc, sl st in next dc) around. Tie off.

Rnd 3: Rejoin in ch just to left of any picot, * (ch 2, picot) 3 times, ch 2, sl st in ch just to right of next picot, ch 5, sl st in ch just to left of same picot, * rep from * to * around. Tie off.

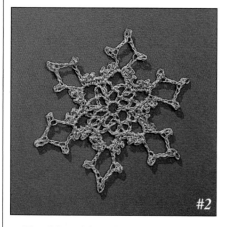

#2

For #2 gold and sliver blend snowflake, chain 6, join with sl st to form ring.

Rnd 1: (Sc in ring, ch 4) 6 times, ending with sl st in beginning sc.

Rnd 2: (Ch 4, sl st in next lp, ch 4, sl st in next sc) around.

Rnd 3: Ch 1, sl st in next lp, (ch 6, sl st in next lp, ch 1, sl st in next lp) around, ending with sl st in beginning sl st.

Rnd 4: *In each ch-6 lp work (sc, picot, sc, picot, sc, ch 2, picot, ch 2, picot, ch 2, picot, ch 2, sc, picot, sc, picot, sc), sc in ch-1 sp,* rep from * to * around, ending with sl st in beginning sc. Tie off.

#3

For #3 gold and silver blend snowflake, chain 8, join with sl st to form ring.

Rnd 1: (Sc in ring, ch 3) 6 times, ending with sl st in beginning sc.

Rnd 2: Ch 1, sl st in 1st lp, (ch 7, sl st in next lp) 6 times, ending with sl st in beginning sl st.

Rnd 3: Sl st in each of next 4 ch, (ch 10, sl st in 4th ch of next lp) around.

Rnd 4: In each lp work: 3 sc, picot, 3 sc, (ch 2, picot) 3 times, ch 1, 3 sc, picot, 3 sc. End with sl st in beginning sc. Tie off.

#4

For #4 gold snowflake, chain 6, join with sl st to form ring.

Rnd 1: 12 sc in ring, ending with sl st in beg sc.

Rnd 2: (Ch 4, sk 1 sc, sl st in next sc) around.

Rnd 3: *In lp work (3 sc, ch 4, 3 sc), ch 1, * rep from * to * around. Tie off.

Rnd 4: Rejoin in any ch-4 lp, (ch 10, sl st in next ch-4 lp) around.

Rnd 5: *In lp work (4 sc, ch 4, 4 sc, ch 7, 4 sc, ch 4, 4 sc), sl st in sl st, * rep from * to * around. Tie off.

Rnd 6: Rejoin in any ch-7 lp, *ch 7, 5 sc in same lp, ch 2, in ch4 lp work (sc, ch 4, sc), ch 6, in next ch4 lp work (sc, ch 4, sc), ch 2, 5 sc in ch7 lp, * rep from * to * around. Tie off.

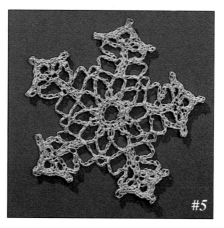

#5

For #5 silver snowflake, chain 10, join with sl st to form ring.

Rnd 1: (Sc in next ch, picot) 10 times, ending with sl st in beg sc.

Rnd 2: Ch 1, sl st in next picot, (ch 6, sl st in next picot) around.

Rnd 3: ch 3, * sl st in next lp, ch 11, sl st in 5th ch from hook, (ch 6, sl st in 5th ch from hook) twice, sl st in same ch where you made 1st sl st, sc in ea of next 5 ch, sl st in same lp as before, ch 3, sc in next lp, ch 3, * rep from * to * around, ending with sl st in beg sl st. Tie off.

Rnd 4: Rejoin in previous ch-3 lp, *ch 5, sl st in 3rd st up stem, ch 5, sc in 1st ch-5 lp, picot, 2 more sc in same lp, in next lp work (3 sc, picot, 3 sc), in next lp work (2 sc, picot, 1 sc), ch 5, sl st in 3rd st of stem, ch 5, sl st in next ch-3 lp, ch 3, sl st in next ch-3 lp, * rep from * to * around. Tie off.

#6

For #6 silver snowflake, chain 6, join with sl st to form ring.

Rnd 1: Ch 1, (ch 3, sc in ring) 5 times, ch 3, sl st in beg ch-1.

Rnd. 2: Ch 1, *sc in next lp, ch 7, sc in same lp, ch 2, * rep from * to * around, ending with sl st in beg sc.

Rnd 3: *Ch 4, sc in ch-7 lp, ch 10, sc in same lp, ch 4, sl st in next sc, ch 3, sc in next sc, * rep from * to * around.

Rnd 4: *In next ch-4 lp work (sc, hdc, dc, tr), ch 4, sc in ch-10 lp, ch 3, picot, ch 3, sc in same lp, in ch-4 lp work (tr, dc, hdc, sc), 3 sc in ch-3 lp, * rep from * to * around. Tie off.

To finish, pin each snowflake to waxed paper-covered cardboard and brush with fabric stiffener.

Silent Night, Holy Night

"Silent Night, Holy Night"—the true meaning of Christmas is celebrated with our tribute to the Star and Christmas Eve. For that very special night at your house we've suggested a glorious make-ahead Christmas Eve buffet complete with a star-shaped mocha torte. The no-sew Christmas pageant costumes we share are simple to make and yet portray the feeling of that evening so long ago. A golden cross-stitched banner and a delicately crocheted star complete this meaningful celebration of that Holy Night.

PHOTOGRAPHER: HOPKINS ASSOCIATES

Christmas Eve Buffet

LEMON-SHRIMP CASSEROLE
GREEN SALAD
MARINATED ORANGE COMPOTE
FRESH STEAMED BROCCOLI
BREAD OR ROLLS
BEVERAGE
MOCHA STAR TORTE

Celebrate Christmas Eve quietly, beautifully, and easily by preparing most of the menu in advance. Lemon-Shrimp Casserole, Mocha Star Torte, *and* Marinated Orange Compote *can be assembled up to 24 hours ahead of time. Early in the day, create a holiday atmosphere with our beautiful cross-stitched* Silent Night Banner *and* Stenciled Star Napkins *plus your favorite china and glassware. About thirty minutes before meal-time, slip the shrimp entrée with purchased bread or rolls in the oven to warm while you put the finishing touches on the compote, toss a green salad, and steam the broccoli. Finally, press lacy chocolate stars into the festive cake for a spectacular edible centerpiece. Instructions for stenciled napkins and recipes are on page 115. Instructions and charts for the banner begin on page 116.*

PHOTOGRAPHER: HOPKINS ASSOCIATES

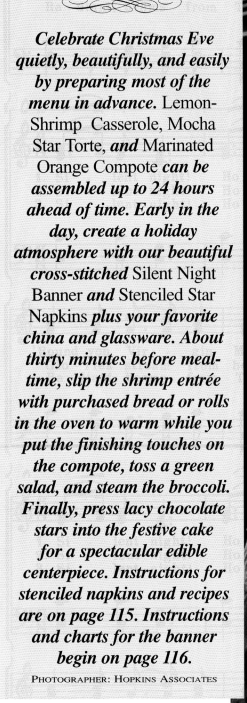

No-Sew Nativity Costumes

When there's so much to do before Christmas, you'll appreciate these easy Nativity costumes that work up quickly and yet portray that night so long ago. Variations of the same simple gown are used for all the costumes. Lengths of fabric and cord, wicker wreaths and ribbon, and metallic paper and acrylic jewels are added to the costumes to make the best-dressed Christmas pageant ever!

DESIGNER: BARBARA B. SMITH ● PHOTOGRAPHER: HOPKINS ASSOCIATES

GOWNS

*A*ll the costumes use the same basic gown. To make the basic gown, which fits children from 50 to 59 inches tall, you'll need 2½ yards of 45-inch-wide fabric. For smaller children, shorten the fabric length. For larger children and adults, increase the length and use 54-inch-wide fabrics. Find the lengthwise and crosswise center of the fabric. Use pinking shears to cut a 5½-inch-diameter neck hole (larger for adults). Cut an 8-inch-long slit from the neck hole down the center back. Slip the gown over the head, lap the lower side edges, and tie at the waist using rope, cord, or a long strip of fabric. Use additional lengths of fabric to create shawls and robes to drape over the gowns.

MARY'S HEADPIECE

*S*imple fabrics in soft blues are the perfect reflection of Mary's gentle spirit. The light blue head wrap is ½ yard of gauze, draped over the head and tucked around the neck. A large triangle cut from a yard of fabric tops the head wrap.

SHEPHERD'S HEADPIECE

*O*ur little shepherd wears a simple headpiece made by draping a ⅔-yard length of fabric over the head and securing it with a 3-yard length of cord. To tie the cord, begin at the back of the head, bring both ends to the front, cross the cords, take the ends to the back, and tie.

ANGEL'S HALO AND WINGS

*A*dorn your littlest angel with a golden halo made by spray painting an 8-inch-diameter wicker wreath with gold metallic paint. Twine 4 yards of glistening ribbon through the painted wreath and tie a bow at the back, allowing the ends to hang gracefully down the back. The wings are easy to make when you start with a large triangle of purchased marble-print paper. Cut the triangle 43 inches tall with a 31-inch base and 45-inch sides. Brush the edges with gold glitter paint. Beginning at the top point and working toward the base, pleat the triangle like a fan, with creases every 1½ inches. Tie the center of the pleated triangle using two 3-yard lengths of gold braid trim, Use ends of braid to tie the wings, base up, to your angel and secure her gown, as

shown in the photograph. To help these wings keep their heavenly shape, staple the sides of the wings together above and below the ties.

KING'S CROWN

*O*ur regal king wears a sheer head drape and majestic gold crown decorated with acrylic jewels. Enlarge the crown pattern, *below,* and cut it from metallic gold art paper. Glue the stones in a decorative pattern using white crafts glue. Fit the crown to your king's head, trim ends if necessary, and staple the ends in place. To complete the headpiece, drape a ½ yard length of sheer fabric over the head and top with the crown. Use fancy sugar bowls, antique vases, or jewelry boxes for gold, frankincense, and myrrh.

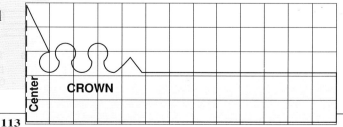

Center

CROWN

1 Square = 1 Inch

113

Silent Night Banners

Magnificent in blue and gold, these cross-stitched banners combine to express the opening strains of one of the most beloved Christmas carols. Each banner is worked in metallic gold threads on a dark blue background, and then lined and trimmed in gold. Nestled in the boughs of the tree, or hung over a doorway, mantle, or buffet, the effect is truly elegant. Charts and instructions begin on page 116.

DESIGNER: JIM WILLIAMS
PHOTOGRAPHER: HOPKINS ASSOCIATES

Lacy Star Doily

This lacy white star doily is a beautiful accessory to your holiday decorating. The entire piece is repetitions of one small circle motif. When it's finished, the doily is spectacular alone or bringing attention to a special centerpiece or holiday decoration. Instructions begin on page 116 and an assembly diagram is on page 118.

DESIGNER: MARY VERMIE
PHOTOGRAPHER: HOPKINS
ASSOCIATES

MOCHA STAR TORTE

INGREDIENTS

1 package 2-layer-size devil's food cake mix
1 6-serving-size package instant chocolate pudding mix
2¼ cups cold milk
1 tablespoon instant coffee crystals
1 8-ounce container frozen whipped dessert topping, thawed
   Chocolate Lace Stars (optional)

METHOD

Prepare cake mix according to package directions. Pour into a greased and floured 10-cup star-shaped baking pan or two 9x1½-inch square baking pans. Bake for 40 to 45 minutes for star, 20 to 25 minutes for squares or until a toothpick inserted in center comes out clean. Cool 10 minutes in pan(s); remove from pan(s). Cool completely on a wire rack.

Cut star-shaped cake in half horizontally to make two layers. Set cake layers aside.

For filling, combine the pudding mix, milk, and coffee crystals in a small mixer bowl. Beat with an electric mixer on low speed until combined. Beat on high speed for 2 to 3 minutes or until mixture is thick. Fold in *half* of the dessert topping. Chill until mixture mounds when dropped from a spoon.

Place bottom cake layer, cut side up, on a serving plate; spread with about half of the filling. Place top layer, cut side down, atop filling. Spread remaining dessert topping on sides. Spread remaining filling on top layer. Cover and chill for at least two hours or up to 24 hours. If desired, garnish with chocolate lace stars. Makes 12 to 16 servings

Chocolate Lace Stars: Melt *chocolate or vanilla candy coating* as package directs. Spoon into a pastry bag fitted with a fine writing tip. Pipe onto waxed paper-lined cookie sheets in star shapes.

LEMON- SHRIMP CASSEROLE

INGREDIENTS

1 pound fresh or frozen peeled and deveined medium shrimp
1 cup long grain rice
2 cups chicken broth
1 10-ounce package frozen peas and carrots
¼ cup sliced green onion
¼ cup sliced celery
1 clove garlic, minced
¼ cup margarine or butter
3 tablespoons all-purpose flour
¼ teaspoon dried dillweed
1¾ cups milk
¾ cup finely shredded Swiss cheese (3 ounces)
½ teaspoon finely shredded lemon peel
3 tablespoons lemon juice
¼ cup toasted almonds

METHOD

Cook shrimp in boiling water just until done, 1 to 3 minutes. Drain and rinse with cool water. Cook rice in chicken broth with peas and carrots until rice is tender, about 15 minutes.

Cook green onion, celery, and garlic in margarine or butter until onion and celery are crisp-tender. Stir in flour and dillweed. Add milk. Cook and stir until thickened and bubbly. Stir in cheese, lemon peel, and lemon juice until cheese is melted and smooth. Gently fold in shrimp and rice mixture. Spoon into a 2-quart baking dish. Sprinkle with almonds. Cover with foil and refrigerate up to 24 hours.

Bake, covered with foil, in a 375° oven for 30 to 40 minutes or until heated through. Makes 6 servings.

STAR NAPKINS

MARINATED ORANGE COMPOTE

INGREDIENTS

2 oranges
¼ cup honey
1 tablespoon lemon juice
¼ teaspoon ground cinnamon
1 cup *each* of three Fruit Options

METHOD

Grate enough peel from one orange to make *½ teaspoon;* set aside. Peel and slice oranges crosswise (halve large slices). Layer orange slices in a bowl. Combine orange peel, honey, lemon juice, and cinnamon; drizzle over oranges. Cover and refrigerate for up to 24 hours.

To serve, drain oranges, reserving liquid. Arrange oranges in bottom of a glass bowl. Top with desired fruits in three layers. Pour reserved liquid over fruits. Serves 6.

Fruit Options: Melon chunks or balls; peeled and sliced bananas, kiwis, or pineapples; sliced carambola (star fruit), sliced or cut up apples or pears; or berries (halve large strawberries); or halved seedless grapes.

STENCILED STAR NAPKINS

Shown on pages 110–111.

MATERIALS

Royal blue damask napkins, or 100% cotton damask napkins and one package dye in desired shade
Stencil acetate; crafts knife
Black ultra-fine point permanent marker
Small stencil brush
Gold metallic fabric paint

INSTRUCTIONS

Dye napkins if desired, following package directions; press. Trace star pattern, *left,* onto stencil acetate using marker. Use crafts knife to cut out star shape.

For each napkin, center stencil in one corner, 2½ inches from tip. Stencil star gold. Stencil an additional star on each side of first, centering each approximately 2 inches from first and 1¼ inches up from napkin edge. When paint is dry, iron napkin on wrong side.

SILENT NIGHT BANNERS

As shown on page 114, each banner measures 6½x30 inches.

MATERIALS

FABRICS
½ yard of 42-inch-wide royal blue 14-count Aida cloth

½ yard of 45-inch-wide royal blue velveteen

THREAD
8 spools of #8 gold metallic braid

1 spool of #8 silver metallic braid

SUPPLIES
Needle

Embroidery hoop

4⅓ yards of gold metallic piping

Royal blue sewing thread

8 yards of ⅛-inch-wide gold metalic ribbon

4 yards of 1½-inch-wide gold metallic ribbon

4 yards of ⅜-inch-diameter gold and white decorative cord

4 purchased gold metalic tassels

INSTRUCTIONS

Cut Aida cloth into two 9x36-inch rectangles. Tape or zigzag edges of fabric to prevent fraying.

For each banner, with 36-inch edge at top, find center of one piece of fabric and center of first chart. (Chart center is at right or left edge.) Begin stitching there.

Work all cross-stitches and backstitches using one strand of braid.

Trim excess fabric from each stitched piece 2¼ inches beyond outermost stitching. If desired, curve ends and cut long edges slightly wavy. With right sides together, use each banner as a pattern to cut a back from velveteen.

Sew piping to Aida cloth, with raw edges even, using ¼-inch seam allowances. With right sides facing, sew Aida to back along piping seam line, leaving opening for turning. Clip, turn, and press. Sew opening closed.

Cut ⅛-inch-wide ribbon into half; attach center of one piece to each end of each banner for ties. Cut wide ribbon into quarters; make bow from each piece and tack one to each end. Cut cord into fourths, tie bows, and attach to ends. Tack tassels at ends.

LACY STAR DOILY

As shown on page 114, finished doily measures 17½ inches from point to point. Skill Level: for the intermediate crocheter.

MATERIALS
Two 174-yard balls of white DMC Cordonnet Special Crochet Cotton, Size 20 (20-gram)

Size 8 steel crochet hook

GAUGE:
After Rnd 1, circle = ¾-inch-diameter.

INSTRUCTIONS

Completed doily contains 121 circle motifs. Each motif is connected to previous ones as it is worked. Work motifs 1–61 (center of doily) as numbered on the chart, *page 118.* Three hatch marks indicate a connection at point where motifs touch; connections are numbered in order worked. Work star point motifs as numbered, connecting last four motifs to doily center.

For center motif, Ch 8; sl st in beg ch to form ring.

Rnd 1: Ch 3 (counts as dc); work 35 dc in ring–36 sts; join with a sl st in top of beg ch-3.

Rnd 2: Ch 1, sc in same sp as join; * ch 3, sk 1 dc, sc in next dc; rep from * around, ending ch 3, sl st in beg sc–18 ch-3 lps.

Rnd 3: Sl st in first ch-3 lp, ch 1, sc in same lp, * ch 4, sc in next ch-3 lp; rep from * around 16 times more, ch 4, sl st in beg sc–18 ch-4 lps; fasten off.

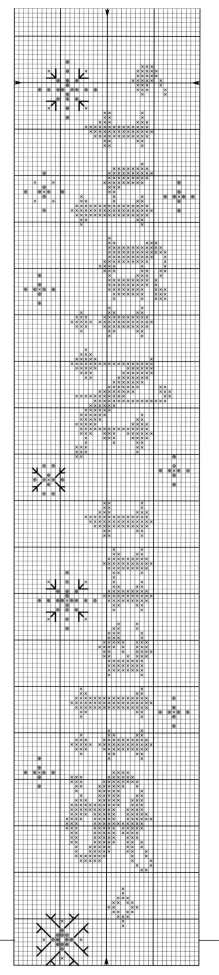

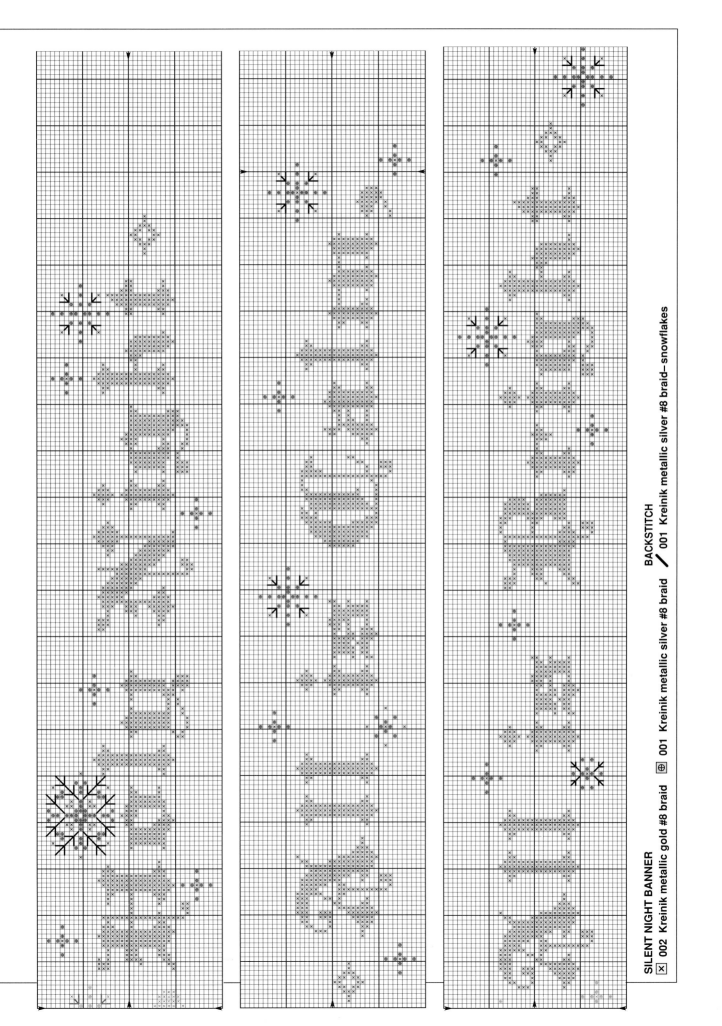

SILENT NIGHT BANNER

☒ 002 Kreinik metallic gold #8 braid   ⊕ 001 Kreinik metallic silver #8 braid

BACKSTITCH

╱ 001 Kreinik metallic silver #8 braid– snowflakes

Work all succeeding motifs as for center motif through completion of Rnd 2.

For second motif, Rnd 3: Sl st in first ch-3 lp, ch 1, sc in same lp, (ch 4, sc in next ch-3 lp) 3 times * ch 2, (drop ch from hook and insert hook into corresponding ch-4 lp on center motif from inside to outside, draw ch-2 into lp–connection made), ch 2, sc in next ch-3 lp on second motif; rep from * twice more, (ch 4, sc in next ch-3 lp) 11 times. Ch 4, join with sl st in first sc; fasten off.

For third motif, Rnd 3: Sl st in first ch-3 lp, ch 1, sc in same lp, (ch 2, connect to center motif, ch 2, sc in next ch-3 lp on third motif) 3 times, (ch 4, sc in next ch-3 lp) 12

times, (ch 2, connect to second motif, ch 2, sc in next ch-3 lp on third motif) twice. Ch 2, connect to second motif, ch 2 join with sl st in first sc; fasten off.

For motifs four–six, work Rnd 3 as est on third motif, following chart.

For motif seven, Rnd 3: Sl st in first ch-3 lp, ch 1, sc in same lp, (ch 2, connect to center motif, ch 2, sc in next ch-3 lp on seventh motif) 3 times, (ch 2, connect to second motif, ch 2, sc in next ch-3 lp on seventh motif) 3 times, (ch 4, sc in next ch-3 lp) 9 times, (ch 2, connect to sixth motif, ch 2, sc in next ch-3 lp on seventh motif) twice. Ch 2, connect to sixth motif, ch 2, join with sl st; fasten off. Complete motifs 8–61, following chart.

For first point of star, work motifs 62–71 following chart and joining center of doily as motifs 69–71 are worked. Complete five remaining points as for first point. Weave in ends on wrong side.

CROCHET ABBREVIATIONS	
rnd	round
ch	chain
st(s)	stitch; stitches
sl st	slip stitch
beg	beginning
dc	double crochet
sc	single crochet
sp	space
sk	skip
lp	loop
rep	repeat
est	established

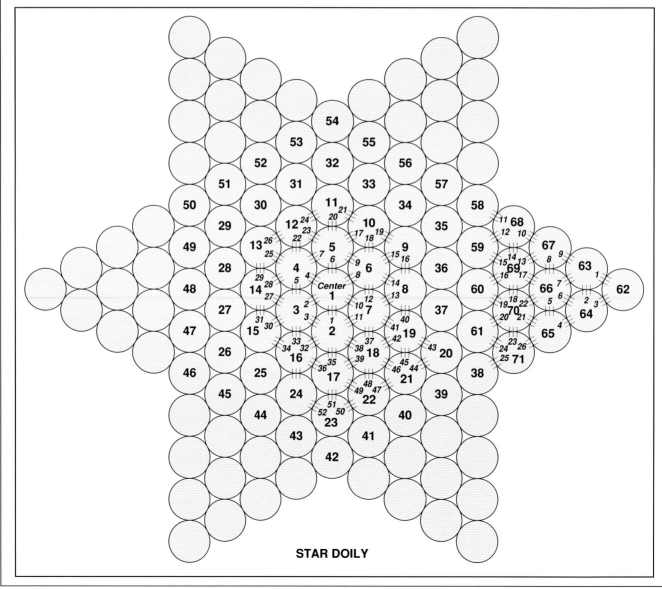

STAR DOILY

Santa Claus Is Comin' to Town

Santa Claus is comin' to town and you'll be more than ready for him with our tribute to the Jolly Old Elf himself. Homemade Christmas cookies and sweet cocoa, created with Santa in mind, are only the beginning. St. Nick Star Ornaments, an elegant Victorian Father Christmas, and colorful Mr. Claus and Rudolph Puppets are just some of the holiday fun to be found in this merry chapter.

PHOTOGRAPHER: HOPKINS ASSOCIATES

Getting Ready for Santa

What could be more fun than making special treats especially for Santa. Our** Quilt Block Cookies **and** Peanut Butter-Graham Cracker Bears **are as much fun to make as they are to eat and leave plenty of room for colorful imaginations. Recipes for the cookies and** Santa's Cocoa Mix **are on these two pages.

PHOTOGRAPHER: SCOTT LITTLE

QUILT BLOCK COOKIES

INGREDIENTS
- ⅓ cup margarine or butter
- ⅓ cup shortening
- 2 cups all-purpose flour
- ¾ cup sugar
- 1 egg
- 1 tablespoon milk
- 1 teaspoon baking powder
- 1 teaspoon vanillla
- Egg Paint

METHOD
Beat margarine and shortening with an electric mixer about 30 seconds or until softened. Add about *half* the flour, the sugar, egg, milk,

After scoring the dough with a wooden skewer, paint the cookies with Egg Paint. When the cookies are baked, the egg mixture becomes shiny and the score lines separate slightly, resembling the seams of a pieced quilt.

Gather with special friends to prepare the cookies for Santa's arrival. No two cookies will ever be alike!

baking powder, vanilla, and dash *salt*. Beat until combined. Beat or stir in remaining flour. Divide dough in half. Cover; chill about 3 hours or until easy to handle.

Roll half of the dough on a lightly floured surface to a ¼-inch thickness. Cut into 4-inch squares. Use a skewer and ruler to score quilt patterns. Use Egg Paint to color in sections.

Bake in a 350° oven for 15 minutes or until done. Cool on cookie sheet 2 to 3 minutes. Remove cookies and cool on a wire rack. Makes about 24.

Egg Paint: Beat together one *egg yolk* and 1 teaspoon *water* in a small bowl. Divide mixture among 3 or 4 small bowls. Add 2 or 3 drops of a different *food coloring* to each bowl; mix well. Paint on unbaked cookies with a small, clean paintbrush. If the colored mixtures thicken while standing, stir in water one drop at a time.

SANTA'S COCOA MIX

INGREDIENTS
- 1   8-quart package (about 10 cups) nonfat dry milk powder
- 1   16-ounce package (about 4¾ cups) sifted powdered sugar
- 1¾ cups unsweetened cocoa powder
- 1½ cups instant malted milk powder
- 1   6-ounce jar (1¾ cups) powdered nondairy creamer
- Marshmallows or whipped cream (optional)

METHOD
Combine nonfat dry milk powder, powdered sugar, unsweetened cocoa powder, instant malted milk powder, and nondairy creamer in a large bowl. Stir until thoroughly combined. Store cocoa mixture in an airtight container. Makes about 16 cups or enough for 48 (8-ounce) servings.

For each individual serving, place ⅓ cup cocoa mixture in a mug; add ¾ cup *boiling water*. Stir to dissolve. Top with marshmallows or a dollop of whipped cream.

PEANUT BUTTER-GRAHAM CRACKER BEARS

INGREDIENTS
- ½   cup peanut butter
- ¼   cup margarine or butter
- ¼   cup shortening
- ⅔   cup granulated sugar
- ¼   cup packed brown sugar
- ¾   teaspoon baking soda
- 1   egg
- ½   teaspoon vanilla
- 1   cup all-purpose flour
- ½   cup finely crushed graham crackers (7 cracker squares)
- Miniature semisweet chocolate pieces
- Frosting (optional)

METHOD
Beat peanut butter, margarine or butter, and shortening in a large mixing bowl with an electric mixer on medium to high speed for 30 seconds. Add granulated sugar, brown sugar, and baking soda; beat until combined.

Beat in as much of the flour and cracker crumbs as you can with the mixer on medium speed, scraping sides of bowl occasionally. Stir in any remaining flour and crumbs with a wooden spoon.

For each bear cookie, shape some of the dough into one 1¼-inch ball (for body), one ¾-inch ball (for head), three balls slightly smaller than ¼ inch (for nose and ears), two 1½x½-inch logs (for arms), and two 1¼x¾-inch logs (for legs).

Flatten the 1¼-inch ball for body to a 1¾-inch round on an ungreased cookie sheet. Attach the ¾-inch ball for the head; flatten to a 1¼-inch round. Attach the small balls to the head for nose and ears. Attach the 1½-inch logs for arms and the 1¼-inch logs for legs.

Decorate bears before baking by pressing in chocolate pieces, point side up, for eyes. For paws, press chocolate pieces, point side down, onto ends of arms and legs. Bake in a 325° oven for 15 to 18 minutes or until edges are lightly browned. Cool on cookie sheet 2 to 3 minutes. Remove cookies and cool on a wire rack. Add colorful frosting trims, if desired. Makes about 20 bears.

Assemble Peanut Butter-Graham Cracker Bears on an ungreased cookie sheet, flattening the balls slightly.

Sprightly Santas

Stitched on plastic canvas, our sprightly Santas bring festive holiday fun as package ties or door decorations. Quick to stitch and just as easy to finish, there will be plenty of time to create a Santa for everyone on your shopping list. The chart and instructions for our cheery fellow are on page 126.

DESIGNER: CAROLE RODGERS
PHOTOGRAPHER: HOPKINS ASSOCIATES

St. Nick Star Ornaments

Let these happy Santas play among the tree boughs this season and watch the smiles they bring to little faces. Hanging onto the branches from twisted paper ropes, they're cleverly crafted from quilted fabric with wooden heart faces and fluffy woolen beards. Make a few for your tree—they'll be the kids' favorites year after year. Pattern and complete instructions begin on page 126.

DESIGNER: JEFF JULSETH
PHOTOGRAPHER: HOPKINS ASSOCIATES

Victorian Father Christmas

Our exquisite Father Christmas is delightfully detailed, down to the twinkle in his eye and the tiny pearl buttons on his shirt. He's dressed in fine fabrics in shades of peach and cream and wears a kindly expression carefully painted onto his face. Craft him early to enjoy throughout the holidays, and if you just can't pack him away at season's end, he'll be pleased to be a part of your home all year.
Instructions and patterns begin on page 127.

DESIGNER: SUSAN CAGE-KNOCH ● PHOTOGRAPHER: HOPKINS ASSOCIATES

Mr. Claus and Rudolph Puppets

Even Santa can't resist taking a break to play with these spectacular Christmas puppets. This cleverly designed Santa, resembling the big guy himself, and his reindeer partner, are made from velour and work well on hands both big and small. They make great gifts, but it's even better to make them ahead of time so little ones can put on their very own Christmas play for the family. Durable and well made, they'll last for many performances. Instructions and patterns begin on page 132.

DESIGNER: CONSTANCE LARGE ● PHOTOGRAPHER: HOPKINS ASSOCIATES

Simple Santa Jewelry

Help spread good cheer this holiday season by sporting Santa on a necklace, pin, or hairbow—just right for either mother or daughter. Our Santa head is made from bakable clay using basic shapes and simple instructions. After the clay is baked, it's ready to become a favorite Christmas accessory by attaching it to a bow or jewelry finding. Instructions for this jolly jewelry begin on page 137.

DESIGNER: BARBARA B. SMITH ● PHOTOGRAPHER: HOPKINS ASSOCIATES

Kris Kringle and Friends

After your child's been so good all year, why not make a very special shirt for him or her to wear while anticipating Santa's long-awaited visit? Santa and his animal friends are simple to paint on a white sweatshirt using fabric paints, paint pens, and our pattern on page 138. Complete painting instructions begin on page 137.

DESIGNER: SUSAN CAGE-KNOCH
PHOTOGRAPHER: HOPKINS
ASSOCIATES

125

SPRIGHTLY SANTAS

As shown on page 122.

MATERIALS *for one Santa*

FABRICS

8x4½-inch piece of 14-count clear perforated plastic
8x4-inch piece of red felt
8x4-inch piece of green felt

THREADS

Cotton embroidery floss in colors listed in key
#8 metallic braid in color listed in key

SUPPLIES

Needle
Pencil; crafts glue
Scissors
⅔ yard of ⅞-inch-wide green grosgrain ribbon (optional)
1 yard of ⅛-inch-wide red satin ribbon (optional)
Three ½-inch-diameter jingle bells (optional)

INSTRUCTIONS

Find center of chart and center of plastic; begin stitching there. Use two plies of floss or one strand of braid to work cross-stitches. Use one ply to work backstitches.

Trim away excess plastic one square beyond the stitching line. Center and glue stitched piece on red felt. Trim away excess felt a scant ⅛ inch beyond plastic. Center and glue atop green felt. Trim away excess felt a scant ⅛ inch beyond red felt.

Cut a 4-inch piece of braid and thread into needle. Take a small stitch in green felt ¼ inch below top of ornament. Knot ends together. *Or,* fold green ribbon in half, forming a loop at fold by crossing the ends 4 inches below fold. Stitch felt behind hat to point where ribbon ends cross. Fold red ribbon into a multi-looped bow. Tack red ribbon and jingle bells to green ribbon just above hat.

ST. NICK STAR ORNAMENTS

As shown on page 122, finished ornaments measure 6½x6¼ inches.

MATERIALS *for one Santa*

Tracing paper
12x6-inch piece of red plaid quilted fabric
15-inch-long piece of brown twisted paper wire
Ecru embroidery floss
Tapestry needle
Polyester fiberfill
⅞-inch-wide wood heart
Pale peach acrylic paint
Small paintbrush
4-inch-long piece of natural white braided wool doll hair
Crafts glue
Black fine-point permanent marker
Seven assorted buttons
Two ¾x6-inch strips of fabric in different red and green prints
⅜-inch-diameter gold jingle bell

INSTRUCTIONS

Trace pattern, *opposite;* cut out. Cut two stars from quilted fabric,

Bend twisted paper wire to form a three-quarter circle. Bend a small loop into each end.

Pin quilted stars together with wrong sides facing. At each X insert one end of twisted paper wire and pin in place. Thread tapestry needle with 6 plies of ecru embroidery floss. Begin working blanket

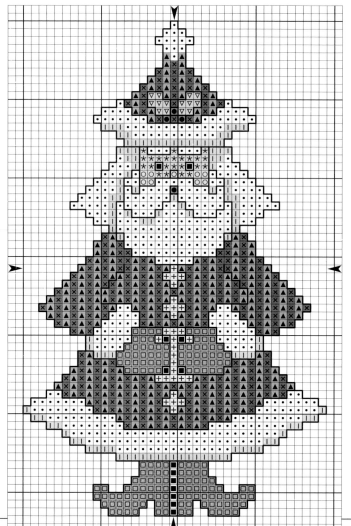

SPRIGHTLY SANTA

SPRIGHTLY SANTA

ANCHOR		DMC	
002	·	000	White
352	▢	300	Mahogany
403	■	310	Black
9046	●	321	Christmas red
398	❘	415	Pearl gray
923	▲	699	Dark Christmas green
228	▽	700	Medium Christmas green
024	○	776	Pink
043	✕	815	Garnet
1011	✱	948	Peach
	✛	002	Kreinik gold metallic #8 braid

BACKSTITCH

403	╱	310 Black – all stitches

Stitch count: 63 high x 39 wide

Finished design sizes:
14-count fabric – 4½ x 2¾ inches

stitch around perimeter, spacing stitches ¼ inch apart and ¼ inch deep, and securing ends of wire. Before completing stitching, stuff lightly with fiberfill. Hide floss ends between layers.

Paint wood heart with peach paint. When dry, glue heart upside down to star with point of heart 1 inch from star top. Cut two ¾-inch-long pieces from wool braid. Unbraid, stretch, and fluff one piece to measure 3 inches long. Glue piece around pointed end of heart for hair. Cut remaining wool braid piece in half, fluff, and glue one piece to each side of heart to complete hair. Next, cut two 1¼-inch pieces of braid. Fluff and glue to lower half of heart for beard. Trim hair and beard as desired. Use marker to make two dot eyes ¼ inch apart.

Use floss to sew six buttons to ornament front, referring to photograph, *page 122,* as a guide. Using a half knot, tie fabric strips onto handle, one atop the other. Sew a button to knot leaving a 6-inch-long floss tail. Thread jingle bell onto floss end and knot in place 1¼ inches from button.

ST. NICK STAR ORNAMENT

Center

VICTORIAN FATHER CHRISTMAS

As shown on page 123, doll measures 24 inches tall.

MATERIALS
Graph paper
¾ yard of 45-inch-wide white muslin
1 yard of 45-inch-wide peach crushed satin
1 yard of 45-inch-wide white jacquard
½ yard of 45-inch-wide white natural or fake fur
¼ yard of 45-inch-wide cream moiré faille
9x11-inch piece of coral felt
Spray starch
Ceramcoat acrylic paints: Santa's flesh, coral, green sea, black, light ivory, and cayenne
Stencil brush
Artist's brushes, including liner brush
Tracing paper; transfer paper
Polyester fiberfill
Gold glitter spray
2.5-millimeter round pearl beads
Natural white curly wool doll hair
½ yard of 3-inch-wide ecru pointed-edge heavy lace
¾ yard of 1½-inch-wide ecru heavy lace edging
Three small snaps; small holly sprig
2⅜ yards of 2-inch-wide ecru heavy lace edging
5-millimeter-long pearl teardrop beads
White quilting thread
Threads to match fabrics

INSTRUCTIONS
Enlarge patterns, *pages 129–131,* using graph paper and cut out. Patterns and measurements include ¼-inch seam allowances. All seams are sewn with right sides of fabric facing unless otherwise specified. Clip curves as needed.

From white muslin, cut head pieces, body pieces, arms, legs, soles, shirt neck facing, and bottom shirt facings.

From peach satin, cut the coat front lining, hat top, sleeve cuff facings, and all knickers pieces. Also from satin, cut a 2½x16½-inch

knickers waistband, four 1⅜x7¼-inch knickers cuff pieces, a 2x15-inch hat facing, and a 1½x13½-inch coat back facing.

From white jacquard, cut hat bottom and coat front, back, sleeves, and undercollar. From fur, cut coat collar, a 1½x15-inch hat trim strip, a 1x1½-inch hat point trim piece, two 1½x8-inch sleeve cuff trim strips, a 1½x13½-inch coat back trim strip, and two 1½x6¾-inch coat front trim strips. From faille, cut shirt front, back, and sleeves. From felt, cut mittens.

Before painting, mix each color of acrylic paint with enough water to make it the consistency of light cream. Allow each paint color to dry thoroughly before using next.

Spray head pieces with starch; let dry. Paint head pieces using Santa's flesh. While paint is still damp, brush coral over nose and cheeks using stencil brush. When dry, trace face detail, *page 129,* and transfer it to head fronts using transfer paper.

Paint irises of eyes with green sea. Paint pupils and outer rim of irises with black. Paint area around iris light ivory. Shade area above eyelids with a wash of cayenne. Shade center of each eyelid with a wash of light ivory, blending outward toward corners. Use a small amount of black to shade inner and outer corners of eye. Paint lower eyelid line, inner eye dot, and mouth using coral, taking care to paint each side in same manner so paint colors and lines match when face is sewn together. Shade mouth with cayenne. Paint eyelashes and outline upper eyelid, eyelid crease, and bottom of mouth with black. Highlight each eye with two tiny dots of light ivory. Heat set paint by ironing wrong side of face pieces.

For doll head, sew head front center seam. Stitch head back center seam from top to dot. Sew head front to back, easing as necessary to fit. Turn head right side out and press under ¼ inch along raw edges of back opening. Set head aside.

For arms, baste a mitten to right side of each hand. Sew arms together in pairs leaving tops open. Turn arms right side out and stuff, stopping 1 inch from top. Sew across tops. Set arms aside.

For legs, sew legs together in pairs leaving tops and bottoms open. Matching centers of toe and heel to front and back leg seams, sew a sole to each foot bottom. Stuff legs as for arms. Sew across the tops of legs, matching front and back seams.

For body, sew center front seam. Stitch center back seam from bottom to dot. Matching raw edges, sew legs to bottom edge of body front. Match top edge of each arm to dot at shoulder and baste in same manner. Sew body front to back, sandwiching arms and legs in between fabric. Sew head to body, stitching around twice. Turn head and body right side out and stuff firmly. Slip-stitch opening closed.

Paint feet below boot line using coral. When paint is dry, spray feet lightly with gold glitter. Sew three pearls to each boot at dots.

Cut curly wool into 10-inch-long strands. Using a large needle and a single strand of quilting thread, tack the center of each strand in place. Sew two rows of wool strands to the face between mouth and chin bottom, curving rows up to eye level on each side of face. Tack a strand of wool under the nose for a mustache, and secure ends in beard. Stitch another strand over each eye along eyebrow line. Trim beard and brows as desired.

For knickers, stitch center back seam from crotch to dot. Press under ¼ inch along back opening from dot to waist. Sew center front seam. Sew side seams.

For cuffs, cut 3-inch-wide lace in half. Sandwich each piece between two cuff pieces, matching straight edge of lace to raw edges on one long side; stitch. Turn the cuff right side out with the lace hanging down from cuff. Baste raw edges together. Gather knickers bottom to fit cuff; sew cuff to knickers leg. Repeat for other cuff. Press seam toward pant leg and sew inseam.

Topstitch back opening close to pressed edge. Sew one long edge of waistband to waist of pants. Press fabric under ¼ inch along remaining long edge, turn it to inside, and slip-stitch to seam. Turn under raw edges on waistband ends and stitch.

For shirt, sew center front seam. With raw edges even, baste 1½-inch-wide lace to right side of shirt front around neck. Sew shirt backs to front at shoulders. Sew center front seam of neck facing; zigzag outer curved edge. Sew the neck facing to shirt. Press facing to inside, and topstitch close to the neck edge.

Stitch 1½-inch-wide lace to each sleeve bottom, press seam toward sleeve, and topstitch. Gather sleeve tops to fit armholes and sew sleeves to shirt.

Sew shirt front facing pieces together at center front. Sew each shirt facing to appropriate shirt bottom. Trim seam and clip points. Turn facing to wrong side and press. Sew side seams and sleeve seams. Turn fabric under ¼ inch along center back edges and stitch. Sew three snaps to opening.

Sew three teardrop pearls to each point of bottom shirt front. Sew teardrop pearls down shirt front for buttons. Accent lace collar with teardrop pearls as desired.

For hat, sew each hat bottom piece to a hat top. Press seam allowance toward hat bottom and topstitch. Sew one side seam. Lay the fur trim strip, right side up, along bottom of hat and stitch in place along bottom edge.

Cut a 14½-inch piece of 2-inch-wide lace. Position straight edge of lace, right side up, under top edge of fur. Stitch the top edge of fur to hat, securing lace. Zigzag one long edge of hat facing. Sew the facing to hat bottom, matching raw edge of facing with bottom edge of fur. Sew remaining side seam. Turn facing to inside and tack in place.

Fold hat point trim strip in half; glue. Stitch trim to tip of hat. Sew round pearl beads and teardrop pearls to lace on hat as desired.

For coat, using same procedure as for bottom edge of hat, sew fur trim pieces and lace to bottom edge of coat back.

For coat fronts, sew the fur trim along the bottom edge and position lace in the same manner as for back. Next, baste the lace along opening edges of the coat front, right side up, matching straight lace edge to raw edge of fabric. Tuck bottom cut end of lace under the top edge of fur.

Stitch top edge of fur in place, securing both the edge of lace along the bottom and the bottom end of lace along the opening edge.

Sew the coat front lining pieces to the coat fronts along the bottom edge and the front opening edges. Sew the coat back facing to the bottom edge of coat back. Turn the lining and facing to the wrong side and press. Tack facing to coat back. Sew shoulder seams.

Sew the sleeves to the coat. Sew the fur trim and 2-inch-wide lace to the sleeve bottoms as for the bottom edge of the coat. Sew the cuff facings to the sleeve bottoms. Turn the fabric under ¼ inch along the remaining long edges of the facings. Fold the facings to the wrong sides and tack facings in place. Sew the underarm/side seams.

Sew the fur collar to the fabric undercollar leaving the neck edge open. Turn the collar right side out and baste the raw edges together. Sew the collar to the coat neck with the fur facing the inside of the coat.

Trim the seam allowance and turn the collar to the right side. Tack the collar along the upper part of the front opening. Finger-press collar to lay flat and hide the seam.

Sew seed pearls and teardrop pearl beads to the lace trim in same manner as for the hat. Tack holly sprig to left side of collar.

Dress Santa in the shirt and knickers. Overlap the knickers waistband to fit doll and tack in place. Put the coat and hat on last, stuffing the hat as desired for height. Secure the hat to the head with glue or tacking stitches.

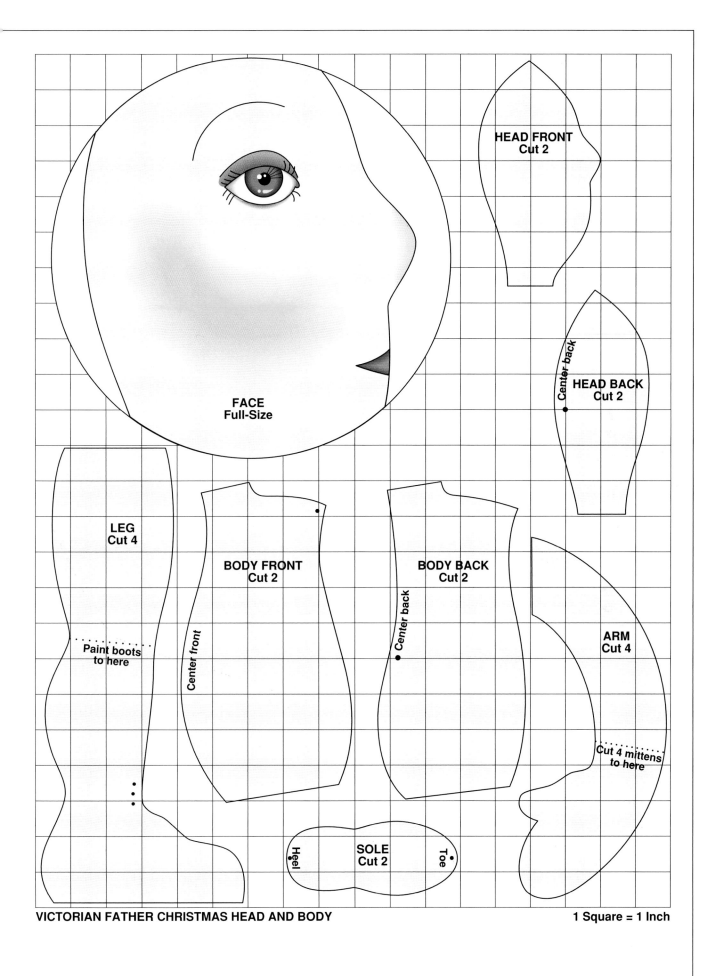

HEAD FRONT
Cut 2

HEAD BACK
Cut 2
Center back

FACE
Full-Size

LEG
Cut 4

Paint boots
to here

Center front

BODY FRONT
Cut 2

BODY BACK
Cut 2
Center back

ARM
Cut 4

Cut 4 mittens
to here

Heel

SOLE
Cut 2

Toe

VICTORIAN FATHER CHRISTMAS HEAD AND BODY

1 Square = 1 Inch

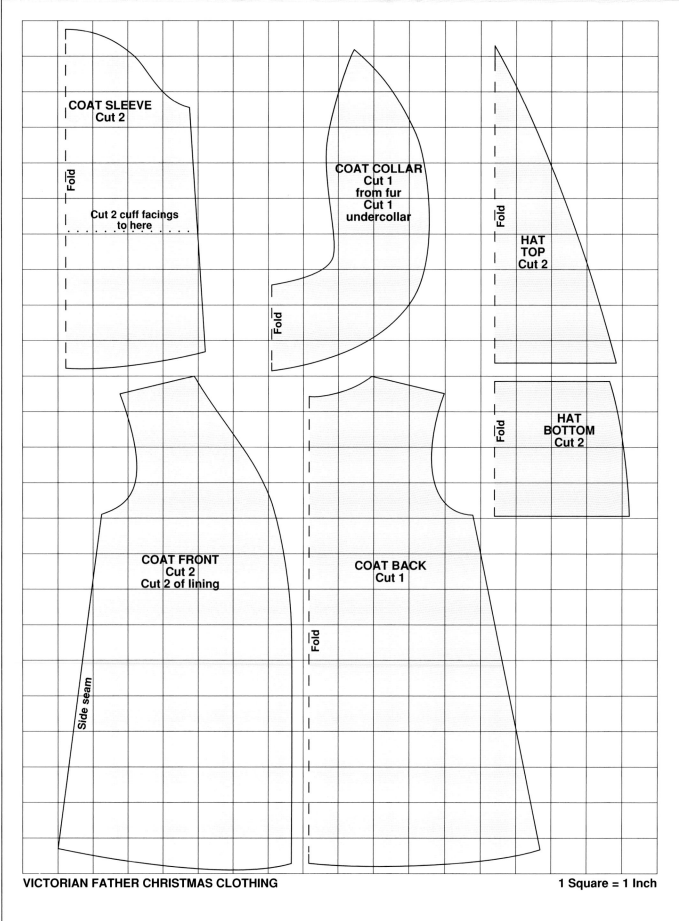

COAT SLEEVE
Cut 2

Fold

Cut 2 cuff facings
to here

COAT COLLAR
Cut 1
from fur
Cut 1
undercollar

Fold

Fold

**HAT
TOP
Cut 2**

Fold

Fold

**HAT
BOTTOM
Cut 2**

COAT FRONT
Cut 2
Cut 2 of lining

COAT BACK
Cut 1

Fold

Side seam

VICTORIAN FATHER CHRISTMAS CLOTHING

1 Square = 1 Inch

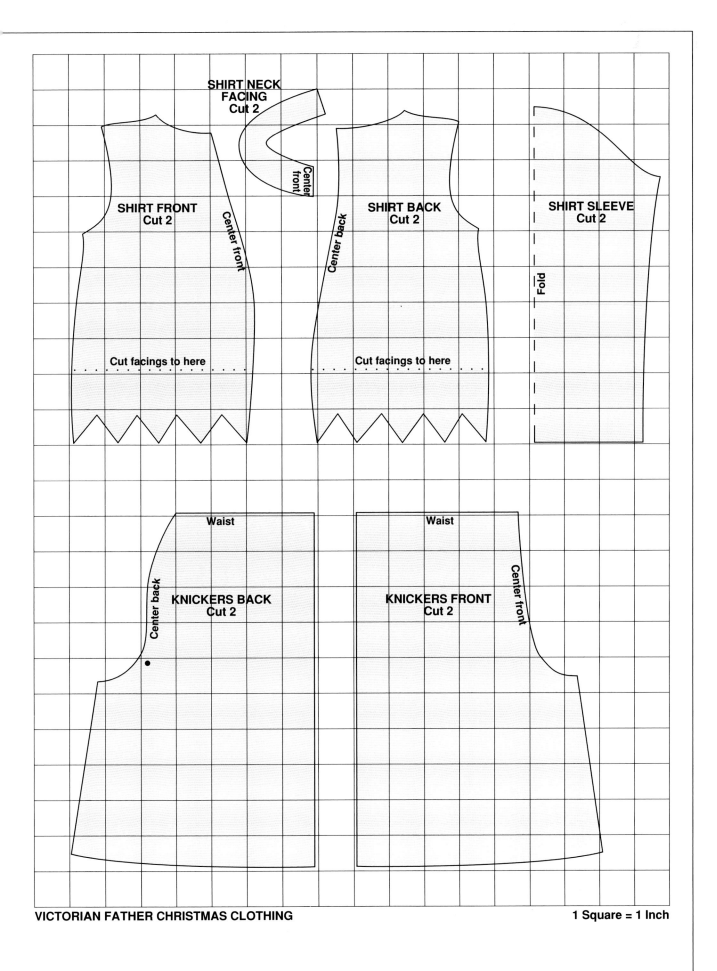

SHIRT NECK FACING
Cut 2

Center front

SHIRT FRONT
Cut 2

Center front

Cut facings to here

SHIRT BACK
Cut 2

Center back

Cut facings to here

SHIRT SLEEVE
Cut 2

Fold

Waist

Center back

KNICKERS BACK
Cut 2

Waist

KNICKERS FRONT
Cut 2

Center front

VICTORIAN FATHER CHRISTMAS CLOTHING

1 Square = 1 Inch

MR. CLAUS AND RUDOLPH PUPPETS

As shown on page 124, Santa measures 20 inches tall and reindeer measures 15 inches tall.

MATERIALS

For Santa

⅜ yard of 45-inch-wide peach robe velour

3x3-inch piece of bright pink robe velour

¼ yard of 45-inch-wide white fake fur with long pile

½ yard of 45-inch-wide red robe velour

¼ yard of 45-inch-wide red and green plaid fabric

¼ yard of iron-on interfacing

15x15-inch piece of black polar fleece

¼ yard of 45-inch-wide white fake fur with short pile

10x22-inch piece of polyester quilt batting

2-inch-diameter white pom-pom

Purchased gold belt buckle for a 1½-inch-wide belt

For reindeer

⅝ yard of 45-inch-wide tan robe velour

3x6-inch piece of white robe velour

⅛ yard of 45-inch-wide brown robe velour

7x12-inch piece of polyester quilt batting

Black embroidery floss

8 inches of ¼-inch-wide green satin ribbon

1-inch-long silver bell

For both puppets

Threads to match fabrics

Graph paper; polyester fiberfill

Black, white, red, and deep pink fabric paints

Fine paintbrush; small sponge

Fabric marking pen; crafts glue

Hot glue gun; glue sticks

INSTRUCTIONS

Enlarge patterns, *pages 133-136,* onto graph paper and cut out. Trace around patterns onto double thicknesses of fabrics placing each piece with arrow running in direction of nap, grain, or stripes. Pattern pieces and measurements include ¼-inch seam allowances. All seams are sewn with right sides of fabric facing unless otherwise indicated. Trim seams and clip points and curves as needed.

To cut out Santa, from peach velour, cut head pieces, hands, and lining. Transfer face detail.

From pink velour, cut nose.

From long-pile fur, cut eyebrows, mustache, beard, and hair.

From red velour, cut legs, hat, pants, and jacket pieces.

From red and green plaid, cut vest pieces. Also cut vest pieces from interfacing.

From polar fleece, cut boot pieces and belt.

From short-pile fur, cut jacket trim pieces. Also cut two 1x5½-inch sleeve trim strips, two 2¼x6½-inch boot trim strips, and one 2x16-inch hat trim strip, with nap running from top to bottom.

To sew Santa's body, sew pant fronts together along center seam. Repeat for pant backs. Apply interfacing to back of vest pieces following manufacturer's instructions. With wrong sides of vest facing right side of pants, Baste bottom edge of each vest piece in place. to placement lines indicated on pattern. Machine-satin-stitch along bottom vest edges and remove basting. Sew darts in pants.

Fold each leg in half along fold line and sew back seam. Turn right side out. Matching fold line to back seam, baste across top. Baste legs to bottom of pants front, aligning fold line on legs to darts on pants. Sew bottom of one peach lining piece to bottom of pants front with wrong side of lining facing right side of legs and pants, sandwiching legs in between. Turn lining to back and topstitch close to bottom edge of pants. Matching edges, baste sides of pants and vest piece to lining, leaving marked opening along one side unstitched. Align neckline and armhole edges of vest to dots on lining. Machine-satin-stitch along edges. Repeat assembly procedure for body back, omitting legs. Sew body front to back, stitching all the way around lining and leaving marked opening unstitched. Turn body right side out; stuff from waist down, working through openings. Slipstitch openings closed.

Sew hand pieces together in pairs, leaving bottom edges open. Clip curves; turn hands right side out, and stuff lightly. Turn bottom edge under ¼ inch and slide a hand over each arm. Slipstitch hands in place just above vest armholes.

For head, lay all pieces atop quilt batting, wrong side down. Stitch around perimeters ¼ inch from edge. Trim batting close to edges of fabric. Sew darts and head back center seam. Sew back to front, leaving bottom edge open. Turn right side out and stuff. Turn under ¼ inch around bottom opening and make an indentation in stuffing at base of head. With puppet body on a hand, push neck projection into indentation. Slipstitch head to body, sewing around three times.

For each boot, sew front seam. With raw edges matching and right side of fur facing inside of boot, sew boot trim to top edge boot. Turn fur right side out and zigzag bottom edge in place. Sew back seam; stitch sole to boot matching front and back dots to front and back seams. Turn each boot right side out and stuff to ankle. Stuff legs through bottom opening. Pull each boot onto a leg and hot glue in place.

To finish head and face, paint mouth red and eyes black with white highlights. Work a running stitch around nose circle ¼ inch from edge. Pull thread to gather edge; stuff nose. Pull thread tight; knot. Slipstitch nose in place at X on pattern. Glue beard below mouth, and mustache between nose and mouth. Using sponge, lightly blush cheeks with deep pink. Turn under ½ inch along top edge of hair piece and secure with hot glue. Position hair on head, centering at back and wrapping sides so top corner meets tip of mustache; glue. Glue eyebrows over eyes.

Continued on page 136

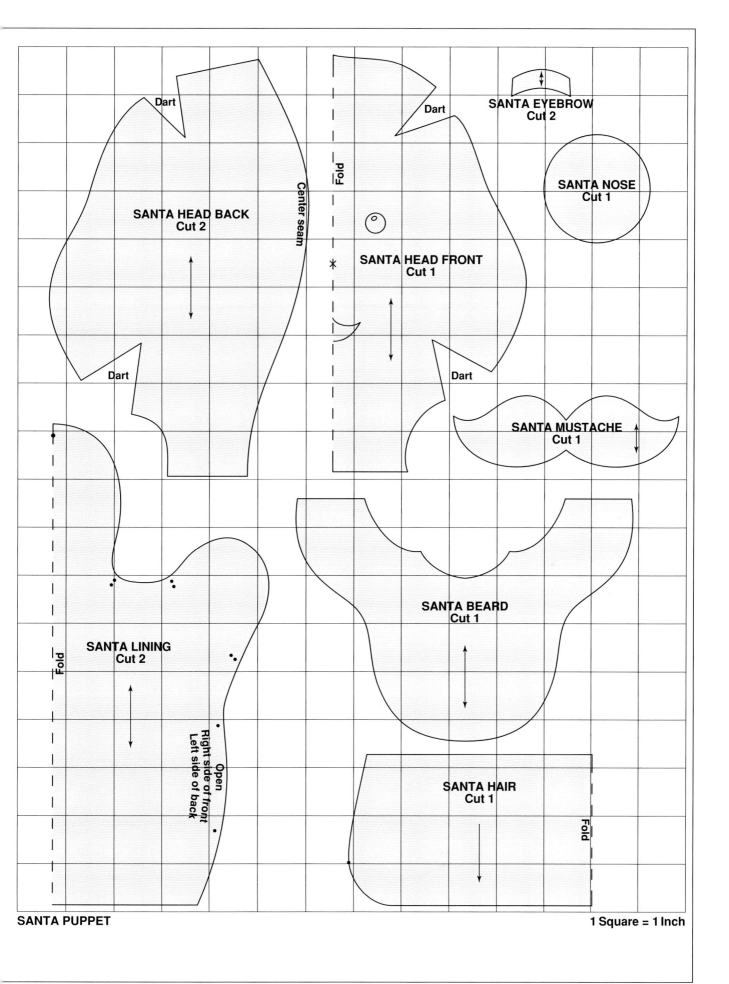

SANTA EYEBROW
Cut 2

SANTA NOSE
Cut 1

Dart

Dart

Fold

Center seam

SANTA HEAD BACK
Cut 2

SANTA HEAD FRONT
Cut 1

Dart

Dart

SANTA MUSTACHE
Cut 1

SANTA BEARD
Cut 1

Fold

SANTA LINING
Cut 2

Open
Right side of front
Left side of back

SANTA HAIR
Cut 1

Fold

SANTA PUPPET

1 Square = 1 Inch

133

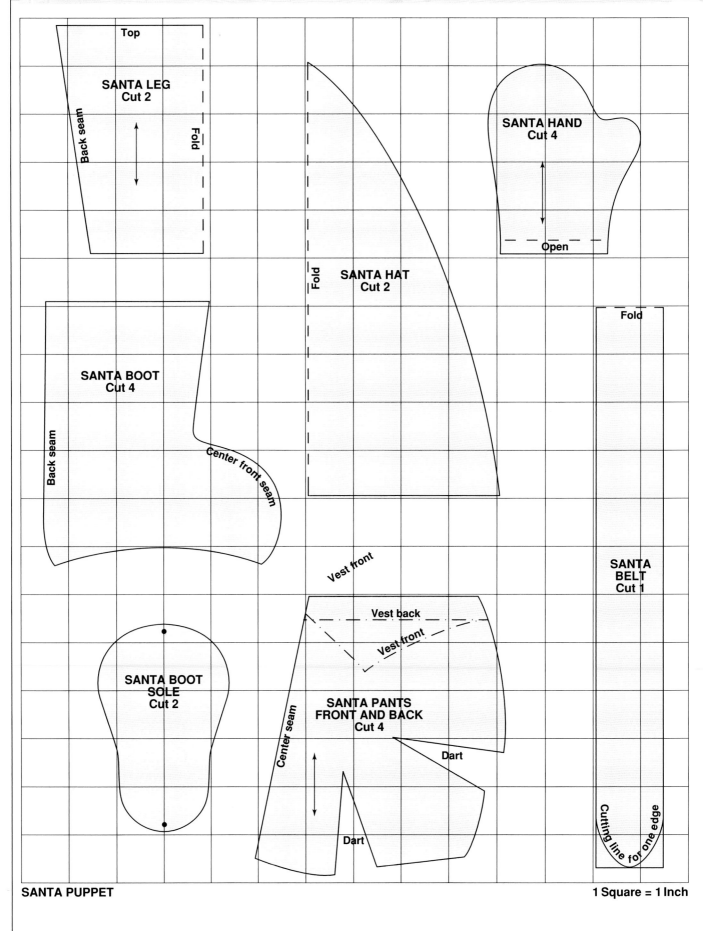

SANTA LEG
Cut 2

Top

Back seam

Fold

SANTA HAND
Cut 4

Open

Fold

SANTA HAT
Cut 2

SANTA BOOT
Cut 4

Back seam

Center front seam

Fold

SANTA BELT
Cut 1

Cutting line for one edge

Vest front

Vest back

Vest front

SANTA BOOT SOLE
Cut 2

SANTA PANTS FRONT AND BACK
Cut 4

Center seam

Dart

Dart

SANTA PUPPET

1 Square = 1 Inch

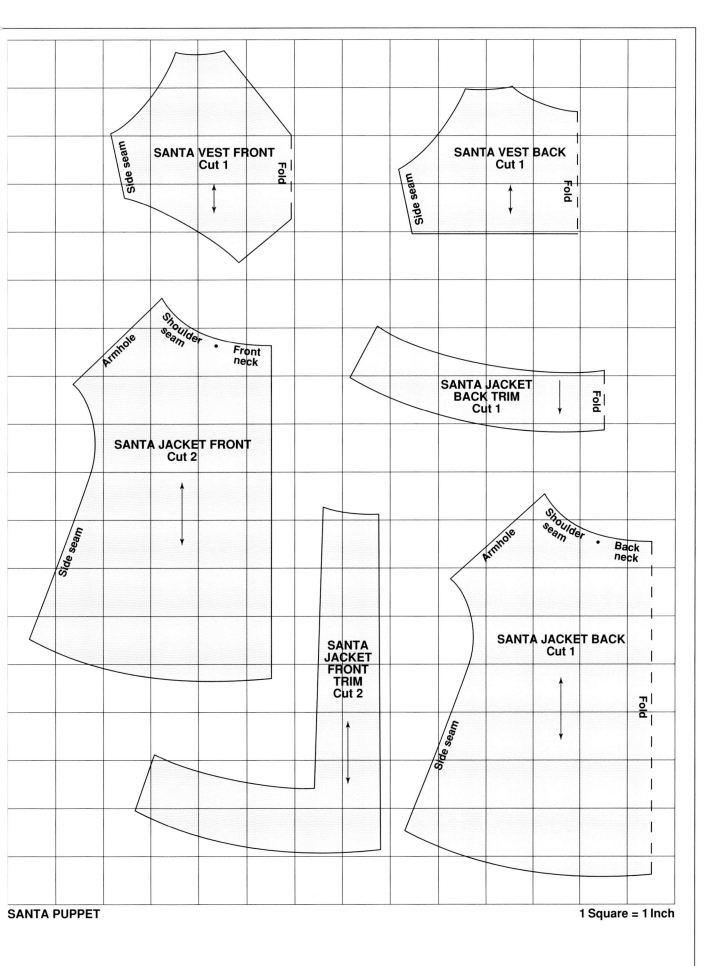

SANTA VEST FRONT
Cut 1

Side seam

Fold

SANTA VEST BACK
Cut 1

Side seam

Fold

Armhole

Shoulder seam

• Front neck

SANTA JACKET FRONT
Cut 2

Side seam

SANTA JACKET BACK TRIM
Cut 1

Fold

SANTA JACKET FRONT TRIM
Cut 2

Armhole

Shoulder seam

• Back neck

SANTA JACKET BACK
Cut 1

Side seam

Fold

SANTA PUPPET

1 Square = 1 Inch

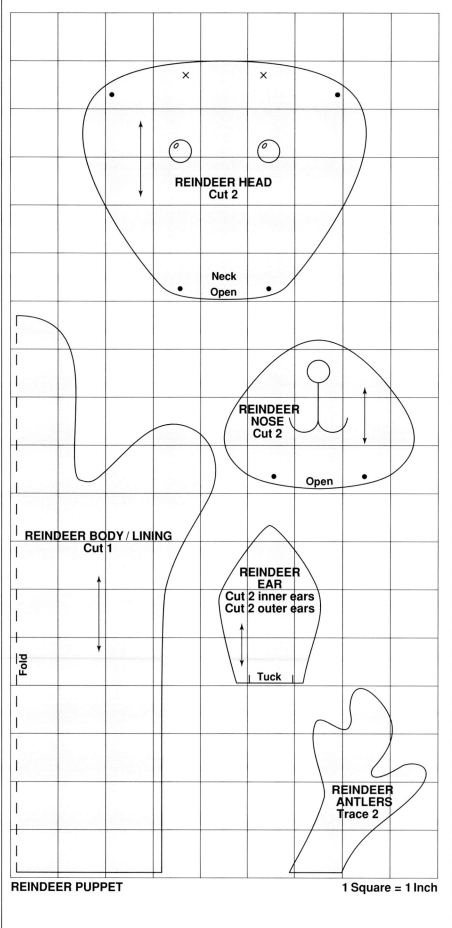

REINDEER HEAD
Cut 2

Neck
Open

**REINDEER
NOSE
Cut 2**

Open

REINDEER BODY / LINING
Cut 1

Fold

**REINDEER
EAR
Cut 2 inner ears
Cut 2 outer ears**

Tuck

**REINDEER
ANTLERS
Trace 2**

REINDEER PUPPET

1 Square = 1 Inch

For hat, stitch one side seam. With raw edges matching and right side of fur to wrong side of hat, stitch hat trim to hat bottom. Turn fur to right side, fold under ¼ inch along raw edge, and slipstitch in place. Sew remaining side seam. Glue pom-pom to point of hat. Slipstitch hat to Santa's head.

For jacket, sew side seams on both the jacket and trim pieces, joining back to fronts. With raw edges matching and right side of fur to wrong side of jacket, sew trim to jacket side and bottom edges. Sew the sleeve trim to sleeves in same manner. Turn fur to right side of jacket and zigzag raw edges in place. Sew shoulder seams. Turn under ¼ inch along neck edge and topstitch.

For belt, glue straight edge of belt strip to center bar of buckle. Put jacket on Santa; secure with belt.

To cut reindeer, from tan velour, cut body/lining, head, nose, and outer ears.

From the white velour, cut the inner ears.

On brown velour, with the straight edge of pattern on cut edge of fabric, trace two antlers. *Do not cut out.*

To sew reindeer's body, sew bottom edges of two body/lining pieces together; turn right side out. Repeat with remaining pieces. With bottom edges even, sew the four body pieces together, leaving bottom edge open. Clip curves and turn body right side out.

For head, stack head pieces together, right sides facing, and lay them atop quilt batting. Stitch around perimeter of head ¼ inch inside outer edge, leaving marked neck opening unstitched. Trim batting close to fabric edge. Turn head right side out and stuff to 1½ inches thick. Repeat for nose and slipstitch nose opening closed. Make an indentation in stuffing at base of head. With puppet body on a hand, push neck projection into indentation. Turn under ¼ inch around bottom opening and slipstitch head to body, sewing around three times.

For **antlers,** fold fabric so each traced antler is on a double thickness of fabric. Sew around each antler on traced line, leaving bottoms open. Trim seam allowances to a scant ¼ inch and clip curves. Turn antlers right side out and stuff. Turn under ½ inch along bottom edges and slipstitch them to head top at Xs.

For **ears,** sew inner ear pieces to outer ear pieces in pairs, leaving bottoms open. Turn under ¼ inch along bottom edges. Tuck ears to indent inner portion, and slipstitch to head top at dots.

To finish puppet, hot glue nose to lower part of face. After gluing, slipstitch to secure. Paint eyes and nose circle black. Add white highlights to eyes. Backstitch mouth using six plies of black embroidery floss. String bell onto ⅛-inch-wide ribbon and tie around neck.

SANTA JEWELRY

As shown on page 125, Santa measures 2¾x1⅜ inches.

MATERIALS

Fimo or Sculpey oven-bakable clay: pale peach, red, and white
Paring knife; garlic press
Powdered blush; small artist's brush
Fine point permanent black marker
Hot glue gun; glue sticks
For necklace
Paper clip; wire cutters
1 yard of ⅛-inch-diameter green and gold cord
Small holly sprig
Two ¾-inch-diameter gold jingle bells
For pin
1-inch-long pin back
⅜-inch-diameter gold jingle bell
For hair bow
½ yard of 1½-inch-wide green, gold, and red striped ribbon
2¼-inch-long French barrette back

INSTRUCTIONS

Knead clay until it is pliable. For *each* Santa face, roll a piece of peach clay into a ball the size of a large pea. Flatten ball to measure ¾

inch in diameter. Also from peach, roll a ⅛-inch-diameter nose; center on face and press gently to secure.

Cut a ½x½x½-inch cube of red clay for hat. Roll cube into a ball. Flatten and shape clay with fingers into a flat triangle measuring 2¼ inches across bottom, 1¼ inches tall, and approximately 1¼ inches along each side. Join sides to form a cone. Slightly flatten cone and slide it over the top of face circle. (Hat will appear too large for face and should stick out on each side.)

Shape hat so point curves to left. Roll a ball of white clay to the size of a pea; press it to point of hat. Roll a piece of white clay into a ⅛-inch-diameter rope; flatten and wrap around bottom of hat for trim. Use tip of paring knife to add texture to white ball and trim.

Press white clay through garlic press to make whiskers and hair. Arrange hair on each side of head, attaching it under edges of hat. Press gently to hat and face to secure. Arrange whiskers to make a beard across face below nose. Press two longer strands horizontally under nose for a mustache. Use two ¼-inch-long strands for eyebrows.

Bake clay heads in a 225° oven. for 20 minutes; allow to cool. Color cheeks and nose with a small brush rubbed across powdered blush. Dot eyes using fine point marker.

For Santa necklace, before baking, use wire cutters to cut a ½-inch-long U-shape from paper clip. Press cut ends into clay at back of hat near top. Tilt loop away from clay so a cord can be threaded through loop. Bake as directed.

Knot cord through loop in Santa. Thread a ¾-inch-diameter jingle bell onto each end of cord. Tie a square knot in cord, securing bells next to Santa's hat. Hot-glue holly sprig to top of hat.

For pin, after baking, hot-glue pin back to back of Santa. Glue jingle bell to white ball on hat.

For hair bow, tie ribbon into a bow and hot-glue to French barrette. After baking, glue Santa to center front of bow.

KRIS KRINGLE AND FRIENDS

As shown on page 125, finished design measures 9½x7¼ inches.

MATERIALS

Purchased white sweatshirt
Tracing paper; pencil
Iron-on transfer pen; waxed paper
Peach, white, orange, pink, green, yellow, and black fabric paint pens
Copper, red, gold, and pearl iridescent paint pens
White fabric paint crystals
Artist's brushes

INSTRUCTIONS

Wash and dry sweatshirt. Trace pattern, *page 138,* onto tracing paper with a pencil. Turn tracing paper over and retrace using transfer pen. Place tissue, ink side down on front of shirt and iron as pen package directs.

Squeeze out a little paint from paint pen onto waxed paper and use brushes to paint Santa's face peach; paint fur, Santa's beard, mustache, eyebrows, and cow's body white. Paint chicken, cow's spots, and hooves copper, use orange for chicken's beak and duck's beak and feet. Paint chicken's comb and wattle, and pig pink. Paint Santa's suit red and holly leaves green. Paint the cow's horns gold, the duck yellow, and Santa's boots and pig's hooves black. Use red to paint duck's heart, cow's knees, and Santa's lips. Use red to blush Santa's nose, Santa's cheeks, and animal's cheeks. While paints are still damp, shade Santa and animals as desired using thinned black paint. Brush white crystals over Santa's fur, beard, and mittens. Also brush crystals lightly over Santa's hat and sleeves.

Use paint pens directly on fabric to make dots and outlines. Make red dots for holly berries. Using black pen, dot all eyes and outline chicken, Santa's eyebrows, nose, mouth, mustache, beard, and boots. Paint tiny hash marks around fur.

Also with black, paint pig's, cow's, and duck's nostrils and smiles. Outline chicken's beak and duck's beak and feet with orange. Outline holly leaves, mittens, and duck's necklace in green; chicken's comb and wattle and pig in pink; and Santa's suit, hat, and duck's heart in red. Using pearl, make random squiggles in Santa's beard. Outline the cow's horns and duck's body in gold and cow's body and spots in copper. Use a fine brush and white paint to add highlights to Santa's boots, all eyes, duck's heart, and the holly berries.

Allow all paint to dry 24 hours before wearing sweatshirt; wait 72 hours before washing.

KRIS KRINGLE AND FRIENDS

Here We Come A-Wassailing

Here we come a-wassailing and what fun it is to get together with family and friends at Christmastime to share festive food and gifts! We've started with a holiday menu featuring a traditional vegetable soup ladled into spicy bread bowls served with a variety of homemade breads. Add a colorful flavored cider and sweet Christmas cookies and the stage is set for a perfect caroling party. We've also gathered some wonderful recipes to make and give as gifts complete with clever packaging ideas that are sure to please everyone on your Christmas list. Come together at Christmastime and celebrate the season!

PHOTOGRAPHER: HOPKINS ASSOCIATES

HERE WE COME A-WASSAILING

Caroler's Holiday Party

STONE SOUP SERVED IN
PARMESAN-HERB BREAD BOWLS
ONION-BACON ROLLS
SWEET POTATO BREAD
TWIST-O-CARAWAY STICKS
RELISHES
APPLE-BERRY CIDER
ONE-FOR-ALL CHRISTMAS COOKIES

After a crisp night of caroling, bring family and friends together for an old-fashioned soup supper. Build the menu around a recipe with origins in the children's story, "Stone Soup." The legend tells of two hungry soldiers who tricked stingy villagers into feeding them with "magic stones" that could turn water into soup. After cooking the stones in water, the soldiers sampled the "soup" and declared it would be even better with carrots. A villager brought forth some carrots. Then the soldiers suggested adding meat for an even tastier soup. Several tastings and added ingredients later, the soldiers and the villagers shared a hearty soup. To create our savory Stone Soup, *ask each invitee to bring a vegetable, pasta, or grain to add to the hearty meat stock. Serve the delicious result in edible bowls with homemade breads and colorful Christmas cookies. And be sure to wear something special for the merry season. Our* Candy Cane Apron *and* Peppermint-Striped Sweater *are just the right touch for that perfect party. Turn the page for more about this delicious menu, holiday wearables, and ideas on how to package our flavorful breads for clever gift-giving.*

PHOTOGRAPHER: HOPKINS ASSOCIATES

Candy Cane Apron

Our cheery apron is perfect for parties or for afternoons spent baking Christmas goodies with family and friends. The candy cane appliqué is assembled from small pieces of fabric, fused in place, and outlined with zigzag satin stitching. Holly with red bead berries, a tinkling bell, and a bow accent the candy canes. Make your own red apron or purchase one from a kitchen supply or craft store. Pattern and instructions are on pages 149–150.

DESIGNER: MARGARET SINDELAR ● PHOTOGRAPHER: HOPKINS ASSOCIATES

Peppermint-Striped Sweater

Create a child's cozy sweater to chase away those winter chills. Ours is knitted in stockinette stitch in Christmas green with a candy cane stripe pattern. Merry jingle bells are used instead of buttons to make any little girl or boy giggle with delight. Knitting instructions are on page 148.

DESIGNER: ANN SMITH ● PHOTOGRAPHER: HOPKINS ASSOCIATES

Heartwarming Delights

Our hearty Stone Soup, *ladled into* Parmesan-Herb Bread Bowls, *will warm both heart and soul. A variety of quick homemade breads, relishes, and* Apple-Berry Cider *complete the delicious menu. We've packaged our* Onion-Bacon Rolls, Sweet Potato Bread, *and* Twist-o-Caraway Sticks *in clever* No-Sew Gift Bags *created from Christmas print fabrics to give as gifts. The bags are constructed using fusible webbing and glue. Instructions and diagrams for the no-sew bags and all recipes begin on page 150.*

DESIGNER: MARGARET SINDELAR
PHOTOGRAPHER: HOPKINS ASSOCIATES

Jester Jar Covers and Yummy Treats

Dressing goodies in their finest, these whimsical Jester Jar Covers *can be made the right size for almost any jar. They solve the wrapping problem and become welcome gifts themselves. Tuck* Kiwi-Pear Preserves *or* Rhubarb-Raspberry Jam *inside small jars and pack an assortment of* One-for-All Christmas Cookies *into a larger one. Instructions, patterns, and recipes begin on page 153.*

DESIGNER: MARGARET SINDELAR ● PHOTOGRAPHER: HOPKINS ASSOCIATES

PEPPERMINT-STRIPED SWEATER

As shown on pages 141 and 142. Directions are for child's size 2. Changes for size 4 and 6 in parentheses. Finished chest size, buttoned is 28½ (31, 33½) inches. Skill Level: For the intermediate knitter.

MATERIALS
SUPPLIES
Reynold's Paterna (50-gram or 110-yard skein): three (four, four) skeins of green (928); two (two, three) skeins of black (050); for all sizes, one skein each of red (208) and white (005)

Size 5 and 8 knitting needles or sizes needed to obtain gauge

Three bobbins

Tapestry needle

Size D crochet hook

Five, ¾-inch-diameter jingle bells

GAUGE:
In stockinette stitch and color patterns, 5 sts and 7 rows = 1 inch.

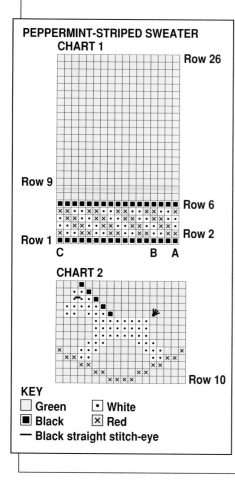

**PEPPERMINT-STRIPED SWEATER
CHART 1**

Row 26

Row 9

Row 6

Row 2

Row 1

C   B A

CHART 2

Row 10

KEY
☐ Green • White
■ Black ☒ Red
— Black straight stitch-eye

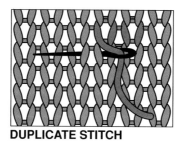

DUPLICATE STITCH

INSTRUCTIONS

Work striped rows of this stockinette stitch sweater from chart below, reading from right to left for right side or knit rows and from left to right for wrong side or purl rows. Carry strands loosely along wrong side of fabric. When changing to a new color, bring new strand from under previous color for a twist to prevent holes. To work rocking horse motif, use bobbins or butterflies and twist strands at color changes. Work black areas of horse motif in duplicate stitch, *above,* after knitting is complete.

For back, with smaller needles and black, cast on 71 (75, 79) sts.

Ribbing, Row 1: P 1, * k 1, p 1; rep from * across.

Row 2: K 1, * p 1, k 1; rep from * across. Rep rows 1 and 2 for 6 times more—14 total rows. Change to larger needles.

Chart 1, Row 1: P across with black.

Rows 2 and 4: K across, rep from A to B, ending at C.

Rows 3 and 5: P across, beg at C and work to A; then, rep from B to A.

Row 6: K across with black.

Rows 7–26: Change to green and work in st st. Rep rows 1–26 until piece measures 16 (17, 18½) inches from beg, ending with a p row. Bind off all sts.

For right front, with smaller needles and black, cast on 33 (37, 41) sts. Work ribbing as for back.

Change to larger needles and work Chart 1 through Row 9 as for back.

Row 10 (first row of chart 2): With green, k 14 (18, 22) sts, k 4 red, k 15 green.

Rows 11–23: Complete rocking horse motif.

Rows 24–26: Work in st st with green.

Work as for back, beginning with Chart 1, Row 1 until piece measures 14 (15, 16½) inches from beginning, ending with a p row.

For neck shaping, in est pat, bind off 4 (6, 8) sts. At the beginning of next k row, bind off 3 sts. Then dec 1 st at neck edge every other row 3 times. Work even on rem 23 (25, 27) sts to same length as back. Bind off all sts.

For left front, work as for right front through Row 9 of Chart 1. K 15 green, k 4 red, k 14 (18, 22) green. Complete as for right front, rev neck shaping.

For each sleeve, with smaller needles and black, cast on 31 (33, 35) sts. Work ribbing rows 1 and 2 until piece measures 3 inches from beg, inc 14 (16, 18) sts evenly spaced across last row 2—45 (49, 53) sts.

Work Chart 1 as for back, including new sts into color pat, inc 1 st each edge every fourth row 11 times—67 (71, 75) sts. When piece measures 11 (13, 14) inches from the beginning, end with a p row. Bind off all sts.

Sew shoulder seams. Center bound off edge of each sleeve to shoulder seam and sew. Join underarm and side seams.

For neckband, with the right side facing using smaller needles and black, pick up and k 67 (71, 75) around neck. Work ribbing for 7 rows. Bind off all sts in ribbing.

For buttonhole band, with right side facing using smaller needles and black, pick up and k 93 (101, 111) sts. Work ribbing for 3 rows. Rib 3 (3, 2) sts, * bind off 3 sts, rib 18 (20, 23) sts; rep from * across for 5 buttonholes, ending last rep rib 3 (3, 2) sts. Rib across next row, casting on 3 sts over each buttonhole. Rib 3 more rows. Bind off all sts in ribbing.

For plain band, with right side facing using smaller needles and black, pick up and k 93 (101, 111) sts. Work ribbing for 9 rows. Bind off all sts in ribbing.

CANDY CANE APRON

Tie jingle bells onto plain band opposite each buttonhole with a double strand of red yarn. For horses' tails, cut two 6-inch strands of black yarn. Hold strands together; fold in half to form a loop. With crochet hook, pull loop through one side of stitch indicated on Chart 2. Pull ends through loop and tighten. Trim ends to ½ inch and fray.

CANDY CANE APRON

As shown on pages 141 and 142, candy cane motif on apron measures 6x9½ inches.

MATERIALS
Tracing paper
10x10-inch piece of paper-backed iron-on adhesive
8x10-inch piece of white cotton fabric
4x6-inch piece of red print cotton fabric
4x6-inch piece of green print cotton fabric
Red cotton apron
10x12-inch piece of tear-away fabric stabilizer
Green and red sewing thread
Twelve 6-millimeter red faceted beads
½ yard of ⅝-inch-wide red satin ribbon
⅞-inch-long gold bell

INSTRUCTIONS
Trace the candy cane outline, red-shaded individual stripes, and holly leaf patterns, *page 149,* onto tracing paper and cut out. Trace around the patterns on the paper side of iron-on adhesive and cut out. Following manufacturer's directions, fuse the candy cane outlines to the white fabric, stripes to the red fabric, and the leaves to green fabric. Cut out. Referring to pattern, position the white candy canes and the green leaves on the front of apron and fuse following manufacturer's directions. Position and fuse the red stripes to the candy canes. Position fabric stabilizer on wrong side of apron front directly under appliqué.

Machine-satin-stitch the leaf edges with green thread. With red thread, machine-satin-stitch the edges of the candy cane stripes where red and white fabrics meet. Stitch again as indicated by the dotted lines on pattern. Then satin-stitch around the outside edges of each candy cane.

Sew red beads as indicated by dots near holly leaves for berries. Tie satin ribbon into a bow around top of bell. Tack bell at intersection of the two candy canes.

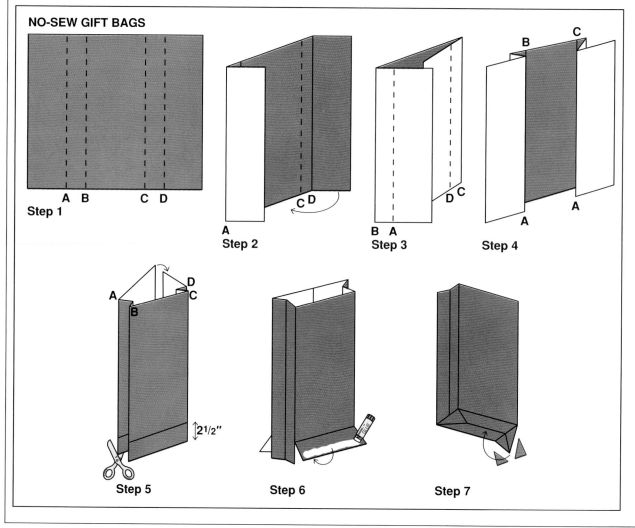

NO-SEW GIFT BAGS

A B   C D
Step 1

A
Step 2   C D

B A
Step 3   D C

C
B
Step 4   A   A

A   D
        C
B
Step 5   2½"

Step 6

Step 7

NO-SEW GIFT BAGS

As shown on page 143, large bag measures 16x6x2½ inches; small bag measures 10x3¾x1¾ inches.

MATERIALS

For large bag

17x20-inch piece *each* **of two coordinating Christmas print fabrics**

16½x19½-inch piece of fusible web

For small bag

13x11-inch piece *each* **of two coordinating Christmas print fabrics**

12½x10½-inch piece of fusible web

For both bags

Pinking shears; ruler; fabric glue

Cord or ribbon as desired to tie bag closed

INSTRUCTIONS

For each bag, sandwich web between wrong sides of fabrics and fuse fabrics together following manufacturer's instructions. Using pinking shears, trim fused fabric to a 16x19-inch rectangle for large bag and a 12x10-inch rectangle for small bag. Determine which fabric is desired for outside of bag.

For large bag, make ¼-inch-long slits along one 19-inch-long side as follows: 4 inches in from left corner for A, 2½ inches in from A for B, 4 inches in from right corner for D, and 2½ inches from D for C (Step 1, left).

For small bag, make ¼-inch-long slits along one 12-inch-long side as follows: 2¼ inches in from left corner for A, 1¾ inches in from A for B, 2¼ inches in from right corner for D, and 1¾ inches in from D for C (Step 1, left). (Slits A, B, C, and D mark bottom of each fold line for assembling bag. The edge with slits becomes bag bottom.)

For each bag, with inside fabric up, press short sides of rectangle toward center along foldlines A and D (Step 2). Open rectangle out, and fold short sides in along fold lines C and D (Step 3). Bring fold A to fold B and fold C to fold D to make side pleats of bag (Step 4).

Open rectangle out and press 2½ inches along the bottom edge to wrong side. Open fold back out and cut slits at A, B, C, and D to fold line. Shape bag, overlap side edges at back, and glue in place (Step 5). Lap front bottom flap over back bottom flap and glue in place (Step 6). Cut each side flap to a point using pinking shears and glue them to bag bottom (Step 7).

After filling bag, tie top with cord or ribbon.

STONE SOUP

As shown on page 143, this recipe can easily be doubled or even tripled if you use a larger soup pot.

INGREDIENTS

1   pound lean ground beef, lean ground pork, or lean ground raw turkey

1   medium onion, chopped

1   clove garlic, minced

4   cups water

4   teaspoons beef bouillon granules

1   teaspoon dried herb, crushed (basil, oregano, marjoram, or thyme)

6   contributed ingredients and additional water specified for each

Salt and pepper

METHOD

Cook ground meat, onion, and garlic in a 5- or 6-quart soup pot until meat is browned and onion is tender. Drain fat. Add the 4 cups of water, bouillon granules, and dried herb. Bring to boiling, reduce heat and simmer 20 minutes, stirring occasionally. If necessary, reduce heat and keep warm.

Meanwhile, calculate total amount of additional water needed for all six contributed ingredients.

Return soup to boiling. Add any fresh vegetables and *all* of additional water for contributed ingredients. Reduce heat and simmer, covered, for 20 minutes. Add any frozen vegetables, pasta, or grain. Simmer,

covered, 10 minutes more. Add any undrained canned vegetables and simmer, covered, 10 minutes. Season to taste with salt and pepper. Ladle into bread bowls. Makes six servings.

Contributed ingredients: *For each 1 cup of fresh vegetables,* (sliced carrots, chopped celery, chopped green pepper, chopped onion, or cubed potatoes), add ¼ cup additional water.

For each 8 to 10-ounce package or 1½ cups of loose-pack frozen vegetables (mixed vegetables, corn, cut green beans, lima beans, peas, cauliflowerettes, or chopped broccoli), add ¼ cup additional water.

For each ½ cup pasta or grain (elbow macaroni, corkscrew macaroni, bowtie, wagon wheel, alphabet-shaped pasta, egg noodles, broken lasagna noodles, broken spaghetti, or for ¼ cup quick-cooking barley or dried lentils), add ½ cup additional water.

For each 8- or 16-ounce can of vegetables (tomato juice; undrained tomatoes, cut up; undrained corn, beans, peas, or carrots), add *no* additional water.

PARMESAN-HERB BREAD BOWLS

It's a good idea to serve these bread bowls with a shallow soup bowl liner, as shown on page 143.

INGREDIENTS

1   16-ounce package hot roll mix

⅓   cup grated Parmesan cheese

1   teaspoon dried Italian seasoning, crushed

1¼ cups hot water (120° to 130°)

2   tablespoons cooking oil

1   slightly beaten egg white

1   tablespoon water

2   tablespoons grated Parmesan cheese

METHOD

Combine flour mixture and yeast packet from hot roll mix with ⅓ cup Parmesan cheese and Italian seasoning in a large mixing bowl; mix well. Add hot water and oil. Stir until dough follows spoon around bowl. Turn dough onto a lightly floured surface. Knead until smooth (about 5 minutes). Cover dough and let rest 5 minutes.

Divide dough into 6 portions and form into balls. Roll each ball of dough into a 6-inch circle. On lightly greased baking sheets, fit each circle of dough over bottom of an inverted, well-greased 10-ounce custard cup or individual casserole. Trim dough at edges of dishes. Smooth edges of dough, pressing against dishes. Brush with a mixture of egg white and the 1 tablespoon water.

Bake in a 375° oven for 12 to 15 minutes or until golden. (If dough puffs up, press it down with a potholder.)

Carefully remove bread from custard cups with a narrow metal spatula. Turn each bowl right side up on baking sheet. Brush insides and rim of each bowl with egg-water mixture and sprinkle with about *2 teaspoons* of Parmesan cheese. Return to oven and bake for 5 minutes more.

Transfer bowls to a wire rack to cool. Store cooled bowls in a clear plastic bag in refrigerator for up to three days or freeze up to 3 months.

APPLE-BERRY CIDER

As shown on pages 141 and 143.

INGREDIENTS

- 8 cups apple cider or apple juice
- 1 10-ounce package frozen red raspberries or frozen sliced strawberries
- 4 inches stick cinnamon
- 1½ teaspoons whole cloves
- 1 large apple (optional)
- Cinnamon sticks (optional)

METHOD

Combine apple cider or juice, frozen raspberries or strawberries, cinnamon, and cloves in a large

saucepan. Bring to boiling; reduce heat. Cover and simmer for 10 minutes. Strain through a sieve lined with 100% cotton cheesecloth.

To serve, pour warm cider into 8 heat-proof glasses or cups. If desired, cut ⅛-inch-thick slices from apple, then cut stars or other holiday shapes freehand or using canapé cutters. Float a shape in each mug of cider and garnish with a cinnamon stick. Makes 8 (8-ounce) servings.

TWIST-O-CARAWAY STICKS

As shown on page 143.

INGREDIENTS

- 1 beaten egg
- 1 tablespoon water
- 1 teaspoon country-style Dijon-style mustard or prepared mustard
- ¾ cup shredded Swiss cheese (3 ounces)
- ¼ cup finely chopped onion
- 2 teaspoons snipped parsley
- 1½ teaspoons caraway seed
- ¼ teaspoon garlic salt
- ½ of a 17¼-ounce package frozen puff pastry (1 sheet), thawed

METHOD

Combine the egg, water, and mustard in a small bowl; set aside. In a medium bowl stir together the cheese, onion, parsley, caraway seed, and garlic salt.

Unfold the pastry sheet. Brush one side generously with egg mixture. Sprinkle cheese mixture lengthwise over half of rectangle. Fold the plain half over cheese, lining up edges and pressing to seal. Brush top of the pastry with egg mixture. With a sharp knife, cut pastry crosswise into ½-inch-wide strips. Twist each strip several times and place 1 inch apart on a greased baking sheet, pressing ends down.

Bake in a 350° oven for 18 to 20 minutes or until light brown. Serve warm. Makes 18 bread sticks.

ONION-BACON ROLLS

As shown on pages 143 and 147.

INGREDIENTS

- 1 12-ounce package sliced bacon
- 1 large onion, chopped (1 cup)
- ½ cup chopped green pepper
- ½ teaspoon dried dillweed
- ¼ teaspoon pepper
- 1 16-ounce loaf frozen bread dough, thawed
- Milk
- Poppy seed, fennel seed, or sesame seed

METHOD

For filling, in a medium skillet cook the bacon until crisp; remove bacon, reserving *1 tablespoon* of the drippings in the skillet. Drain the bacon on paper towels and crumble when cool.

Cook the onion, green pepper, dill weed, and pepper in the reserved drippings until the onion is tender, but not brown. Cool. Stir in the crumbled bacon.

Divide the bread dough into 30 portions. Roll each portion into a ball; roll or pat each ball into a 3-inch circle. Place a scant *1 tablespoon* of the filling in the center of each circle. Bring up the edges of the dough around filling; seal the edges together.

Arrange the filled rolls with seam side down, on a greased baking sheet. Use a pastry brush to lightly brush top of each roll with milk. Sprinkle each roll with a pinch of poppy seed, fennel seed, or sesame seed.

Bake, uncovered, in a 375° oven for 15 to 20 minutes or until the rolls are golden. Serve warm. Makes 30 rolls.

To freeze, prepare and the bake rolls as directed above. Cool thoroughly on a wire rack. Transfer the rolls to a freezer container and freeze for up to 4 months.

To reheat, arrange the frozen rolls on an ungreased baking sheet. Bake, uncovered, in a 375° oven about 15 minutes or until the rolls are heated through.

SWEET POTATO BREAD

As shown on page 143.

INGREDIENTS

- **1** **15- to 16-ounce package nut quick bread mix**
- **2** **teaspoons ground cinnamon**
- **¼** **teaspoon ground nutmeg**
- **¼** **teaspoon ground ginger or**
- **⅛** **teaspoon ground cloves**
- **1** **cup water**
- **½** **cup drained and mashed canned sweet potatoes or canned pumpkin**
- **1** **beaten egg**
- **2** **tablespoons cooking oil**
- **Orange Icing (optional)**

METHOD

Grease and lightly flour one 8x4x2-inch loaf pan or five 4½x2½x1½-inch loaf pans. Set the pans aside.

Stir together the quick bread mix, cinnamon, nutmeg, and ginger or cloves in a large mixing bowl. Add water, sweet potato or pumpkin, egg, and oil. Stir just until dry ingredients are moistened.

Pour the batter into prepared pan(s). Bake in a 350° oven until a toothpick inserted near the center(s) comes out clean. Allow 60 to 65 minutes baking time for large pan or 30 to 35 minutes baking time for small pans.

Cool in pans(s) on a wire rack for 10 minutes. Remove from pans; cool completely on rack. If desired, wrap in clear plastic wrap and store loaves overnight in a cool, dry place for easier slicing. If desired, drizzle loaves with orange icing before serving or giving. Makes 1 large loaf or 5 small loaves.

Orange Icing: In a small mixing bowl stir together 1 cup unsifted *powdered sugar* and enough *orange juice* to make of drizzling consistency (about 1 tablespoon).

Gift label: Store in refrigerator for up to 1 week or freeze for up to 3 months.

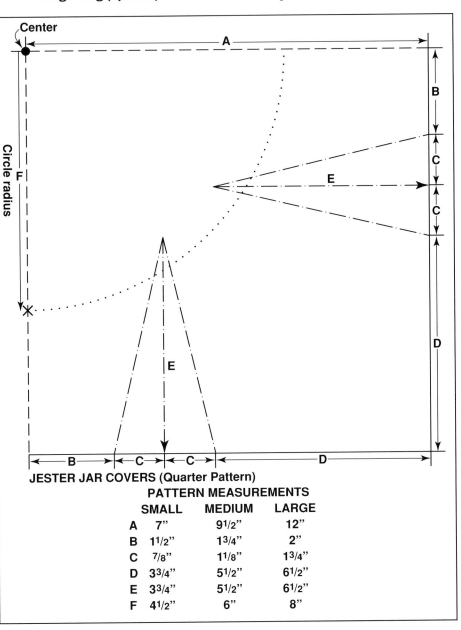

JESTER JAR COVERS (Quarter Pattern)

PATTERN MEASUREMENTS

	SMALL	MEDIUM	LARGE
A	7"	9½"	12"
B	1½"	1¾"	2"
C	⅞"	1⅛"	1¾"
D	3¾"	5½"	6½"
E	3¾"	5½"	6½"
F	4½"	6"	8"

JESTER JAR COVERS

As shown on page 144, the small cover fits a jelly jar, medium cover fits a pint jar, and large cover fits a quart jar.

MATERIALS

¾ yard *each* of 45-inch-wide fabric in two complimentary Christmas prints (makes one large and one medium or small cover)
Ruler
Erasable fabric marking pen
Threads to match fabrics
¼-inch-wide elastic: 11 inches for large or medium cover; 7½ inches for small
Decorative ribbon or cord: one yard for large or medium cover; ⅔ yard for small cover
Four jingle bells in desired size and color for each cover

INSTRUCTIONS

Cut a 24x24-inch square from each fabric for a large jar cover, a 19x19-inch square from each fabric for a medium jar cover, or a 14x14-inch square from each fabric for a small jar cover. Using the diagram and appropriate measurements, *left,* as a guide for each cover, carefully measure and transfer the dart markings to the wrong side of each fabric square. Transfer the circle outline and X to the right side of one square.

Make a ½-inch-long vertical buttonhole at the X on marked fabric square; clip open. Stitch darts on both squares. Press the darts to the left on one square and to the right on the other. Using a ¼-inch seam allowance, sew squares together with right sides facing. Leave an opening for turning. Clip corners and turn right side out. Sew the opening closed and press.

To make circular casing, stitch two circles, one on each side of marked outline, each ¼ inch beyond markings. Insert elastic through buttonhole, overlap elastic ends, and stitch to secure. Sew a bell to each corner. Slip cover over jar. Tie ribbon or cord around elastic casing.

RHUBARB-RASPBERRY JAM

As shown on page 144.

INGREDIENTS

6 cups fresh or frozen sweetened sliced rhubarb
4 cups sugar
2 cups raspberries or one 12-ounce package frozen loose-pack raspberries
1 3-ounce package raspberry-flavored gelatin

METHOD

Combine rhubarb and sugar in a large kettle or Dutch oven. Let stand 15 to 20 minutes or until sugar is moistened. Bring to boiling. Boil, uncovered, for 10 minutes, stirring frequently.

Add the raspberries; return to boiling. Boil hard for 5 to 6 minutes or until thick, stirring frequently. Remove from heat. Add gelatin; stir until dissolved.

Ladle into half-pint freezer jars or freezer containers, leaving ½-inch headspace. Seal and label. Let stand at room temperature several hours or until jam is set. Store in refrigerator or freezer. Makes about 5 half-pint gifts.

Gift label: Serve with toast, muffins, or scones. Store jam up to 3 weeks in refrigerator or up to 1 year in freezer.

KIWI-PEAR PRESERVES

As shown on page 144.

INGREDIENTS

8 kiwi fruits
2 large ripe pears
4 cups sugar
½ of a 6-ounce package (1 foil pouch) liquid fruit pectin
½ teaspoon finely shredded lime or lemon peel
2 tablespoons lime or lemon juice

METHOD

Peel and chop kiwi fruit (should measure about 2½ cups). Peel, core and chop pear (should measure 1½ cups). In a large bowl stir together the fruits. Stir in the sugar. Let stand 10 minutes. Combine the pectin, lime peel, and lime juice. Add to the fruit mixture. Stir for 3 minutes.

Ladle the mixture into half-pint freezer jars or freezer containers, leaving ½-inch headspace. Seal and label. Let stand at room temperature several hours or until set. Store in refrigerator or freezer. Makes about 6 half-pint gifts.

Gift label: Serve with toast, muffins, or scones. Store preserves up to 3 weeks in refrigerator or up to 1 year in freezer.

ONE-FOR-ALL CHRISTMAS COOKIES

As shown on pages 141 and 144.

INGREDIENTS

¾ cup margarine or butter
1¾ cups all-purpose flour
½ cup sugar
1 egg yolk
½ teaspoon vanilla
¼ teaspoon baking powder
¼ teaspoon flavoring

METHOD

Beat margarine with an electric mixer on medium to high speed about 30 seconds or until softened.

Add about *half* of flour, sugar, egg yolk, vanilla, baking powder, and flavoring. Beat until thoroughly combined. Then beat or stir in remaining flour. Do not chill dough unless otherwise directed.

For Spritz, use ¼ teaspoon *almond extract* for flavoring. If desired, after all flour is added, tint dough with *food coloring.* Pack dough into a cookie press. Force dough onto an ungreased cookie sheet. Decorate cookies with *candies or colored sugars.* Bake in a 375° oven for 8 to 10 minutes or until edges are firm but not browned. Remove cookies. Cool on a wire rack. Makes about 42.

For Pecan Snowballs, use ¼ teaspoon *almond extract* for flavoring. After all flour is added, stir or knead in ½ cup finely chopped *pecans, almonds, or walnuts.* Shape dough into 1-inch balls. Place 1 inch apart on an ungreased cookie sheet. Bake in a 325° oven for 15 to 17 minutes or until edges are firm and bottoms are very lightly browned. Remove cookies and cool slightly on a wire rack. Place 1 cup sifted *powdered sugar* in a paper or plastic bag. Gently shake a few warm cookies at a time in powdered sugar. Then cool completely on wire rack. Makes about 42.

For Cherry Nests, use ¼ teaspoon *almond extract* for flavoring. In a shallow dish use a fork to slightly beat 1 *egg white* with 1 tablespoon *water.* Shape the dough into 1-inch balls. Dip the balls into egg white mixture, then roll in 1½ cups very finely chopped *hazelnuts (filberts), pecans, or walnuts.* Place 2 inches apart on an ungreased cookie sheet. Press a *candied cherry half,* cut side down, into center of each cookie. Bake in a 325° oven for 15 to 17 minutes or until edges are firm and bottoms are very lightly browned. Remove cookies; cool on a wire rack. Makes about 42 cookies.

For Candy Canes, use ¼ teaspoon *peppermint extract* for flavoring. For each cookie, shape *1 tablespoon* of dough into a 4x½-inch log. Place logs 2 inches apart on an ungreased cookie sheet. Shape logs into candy canes. Slightly flatten. Bake in a 325° oven about 15 minutes or until edges are firm and bottoms are lightly browned. Cool on cookie sheet for 1 minute. Remove cookies and cool completely on a wire rack. Decorate using *red or white decorator icing* to pipe diagonal lines on top of cookies. Makes about 30.

For Sugar Bells, use ¼ teaspoon *almond extract* for flavoring. Shape dough into two 6-inch rolls. Then roll each dough roll in *red or green sugar* to coat surface. Wrap each roll in waxed paper or clear plastic wrap. Chill for 2 to 24 hours. Cut dough into ¼-inch-thick slices. Place 1 inch apart on an ungreased cookie sheet. Place a *candy-coated peanut or milk chocolate piece* on bottom half of each slice for bell clapper. Then let dough slices stand for 1 to 2 minutes to soften for easier handling. Fold in sides of each slice. Pinch in sides to resemble bell shape. Bake in a 375° oven for 8 to 10 minutes or until edges are firm but not browned. Remove cookies and cool on a wire rack. Makes about 48.

For Holiday Checkerboards, use ¼ teaspoon *almond extract* for flavoring. Divide dough in half. Into one portion, knead ¼ teaspoon *red food coloring*. Into remaining portion knead ¼ teaspoon *green food coloring*. Shape pink and green doughs each into four 10-inch-long ropes. For each checkerboard roll, place one pink rope next to one green rope, then place another green rope on top of first pink rope and another pink rope on top of first green rope. (You will have two checkerboard rolls total.) Wrap each roll in waxed paper or clear plastic wrap. Chill for 2 to 24 hours. Cut dough into ¼-inch-thick slices. Place 1 inch apart on an ungreased cookie sheet. Bake in a 375° oven for 8 to 10 minutes or

until edges are firm but not browned. Remove cookies and cool on a wire rack. Makes about 80.

POPCORN GIFT BAGS

Shown on page 145.

MATERIALS
**Metallic, coated, or heavyweight gift bags in desired colors
Large Christmas cookie cutters
Pencil; scissors or crafts knife
Clear cellophane; masking tape
Paint pens in desired colors**

INSTRUCTIONS
For each bag, draw around desired cookie cutter onto center of one side of bag. Carefully cut out cookie cutter shape along pencil line, being careful to make no cuts outside of drawn lines. Cut a rectangular piece of cellophane slightly larger than cutout. Tape cellophane securely to inside of bag directly behind cutout. Using paint pens, add names and decorations to bag as desired. Allow to dry.

MAGIC POPCORN

As shown on page 145.

INGREDIENTS
1   **3.5-ounce package microwave popcorn or 8 cups popped popcorn
Chocolate-Lover's Mix, Cheese-Tomato Mix, or Easy Herb Seasoning**

METHOD
Prepare popcorn according to package directions. Immediately add desired flavoring mix to popcorn in microwave popping bag or conventionally popped popcorn in a paper bag. Close bag and shake to coat. Makes 6 to 8 servings.

Chocolate-Lover's Mix: Combine 1 cup *milk chocolate pieces,* ½ cup *walnut pieces,* and 2 tablespoons *instant malted milk powder* or *presweetened cocoa mix.*

Cheese-Tomato Mix: Combine 2 tablespoons grated *Parmesan cheese* and half of a single-serving size envelope (4 teaspoons) *instant tomato soup mix.*

Easy Herb Seasoning: Use 1 teaspoon desired dry *salad dressing mix* such as ranch dressing, ranch dressing with bacon, or Italian dressing.

NUTTY NIBBLE MIX

As shown on page 145.

INGREDIENTS
⅓   **cup margarine or butter**
1   **tablespoon soy sauce**
¾   **teaspoon chili powder**
⅛   **teaspoon garlic powder**
⅛   **teaspoon ground red pepper**
3   **cups bite-size corn-and-rice square cereal**
1   **3-ounce can chow mein noodles**
1   **cup peanuts**
1   **cup shelled raw pumpkin seeds**

METHOD
Mix margarine or butter, soy sauce, chili powder, garlic powder, and red pepper in a small saucepan. Cook and stir until margarine or butter melts.

Mix cereal, chow mein noodles, peanuts, and pumpkin seeds in a roasting pan. Drizzle margarine mixture over noodle mixture; toss to coat.

Bake at 300° for 30 minutes, stirring every 10 minutes. Spread on foil to cool. Store in an airtight container. Makes 12 to 15 servings.

RAINBOW POPCORN

As shown on page 145.

10 **cups popped popcorn**
1   **cup margarine or butter**
¾   **cup sugar**
1   **3-ounce package desired flavor gelatin**
3   **tablespoons water**
1   **tablespoon light corn syrup**

METHOD

Remove all unpopped kernels from popped corn. Place in a greased 17x12x2-inch baking pan. Keep warm in a 300° oven while making syrup mixture.

Butter bottom and sides of a heavy 2-quart saucepan. Combine margarine or butter, sugar, gelatin, water, and corn syrup. Cook mixture over medium heat until boiling, stirring constantly. Clip a candy thermometer to side of pan.

Continue cooking over medium heat for about 20 minutes, stirring constantly until thermometer registers 255° (hard-ball stage). Pour syrup mixture over popcorn and stir gently to coat popcorn.

Bake in a 300° oven for 5 minutes. Stir once and bake for 5 minutes more. Turn popcorn mixture onto a large piece of foil. Cool completely. Break popcorn mixture into clusters. Store in an airtight container in a cool, dry place. Makes about 10 cups.

JEWELED TINS

As shown on pages 146–147, it takes about 22½ inches of trim to go around a can once, approximately 1 yard to wrap a handle, 1½ yards for a large bow at base of handle, and 3 to 4 yards of wide ribbon for large bow on lid.

MATERIALS

18-millimeter round acrylic mirrors
18-millimeter red acrylic flower-shaped jewels
4-millimeter gold beads; crafts glue
22x11-millimeter green leaf-shaped jewels
7-inch-diameter colored cans with handles and lids, in desired heights
Red, green, and metallic braids and trims
Wide ribbons
Gift tags; large jingle bells
Thin florist's wire

INSTRUCTIONS

For jeweled can, glue a flower jewel atop an acrylic mirror. Glue a gold bead to center of each flower. Arrange groups of one mirrored flower and two leaves on top of lid, referring to photograph, *pages 146-147.* When leaves and flowers are spaced as desired, glue in place. Repeat pattern around base of tin, using additional jewels, mirrors, and beads. If desired, wrap trim around handle and tie loopy bows made from trim at sides of handle.

For remaining cans, glue trims around bases of cans and edges of lids as desired. Make a large ribbon bow for each lid. Wire a jingle bell to bow if desired. Wrap handles with remaining trims.

Use a scrap of trim to tie a gift tag to handle of each decorated can.

EASY SOFT PRETZELS

As shown on pages 146–147.

INGREDIENTS

1   10-ounce package refrigerated pizza dough
1   beaten egg
1   tablespoon water
Coarse salt, onion salt, sesame seed, or poppy seed

METHOD

Unroll pizza dough onto an 18-inch piece of lightly floured waxed paper. Roll dough into a 16x10-inch rectangle. Cut dough into ten 1-inch-wide strips.

Shape each strip of dough into a circle, overlapping about 4 inches from each end and leaving ends free. Taking one end of dough into each hand, twist at point where dough overlaps. Carefully lift each end across to edges of circle opposite it. Tuck ends under to seal. Repeat with remaining strips. Place pretzels on an ungreased baking sheet, 1 inch apart.

Stir together egg and water. Brush the pretzels with the egg mixture. Sprinkle with salt, onion salt, sesame seed, or poppy seed. Bake in a 350° oven for 15 to 17 minutes or until light golden. Makes 10 pretzels.

HOLLY TOWEL AND BREAD CLOTH

As shown on page 146-147.

MATERIALS

FABRICS *for towel*
½ yard of ⅞-inch-wide 14-count white Aida banding with red trim
Purchased red, white, or green guest towel
For bread cloth
18x18-inch piece of 18-count red, white, or green Davosa fabric
THREADS
Cotton embroidery floss in colors listed in keys
Blending filament in colors listed in key
SUPPLIES
Needle
Embroidery hoop
White sewing thread

INSTRUCTIONS

For towel, tape or zigzag ends of banding to prevent fraying. With long edge at top, find center of banding. Count four squares to the right; begin stitching left edge of first holly motif there.

Work blended needle as specified on chart. Work backstitches and lazy daisy stitches using two plies of floss. Stitch three more motifs, one to the right of the first and two to the left, separating each with eight squares.

Center banding on one end of towel and trim to width of towel plus 1 inch. Turn under ½ inch along each cut end and pin. Machine-sew banding to towel.

For bread cloth, machine-zigzag around fabric, ¾ inch from edges. In one corner, measure 1¼ inches from zigzag stitching; begin stitching center berry of the design there. Work blended needle as specified in key over two threads of fabric. Use two plies of floss to work backstitches and lazy daisy stitches.

Repeat motif in each of the remaining three corners of fabric. For fringe, remove threads between cut edge to machine stitching.

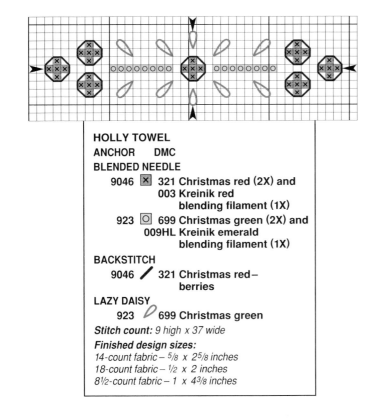

HOLLY TOWEL

ANCHOR		DMC
BLENDED NEEDLE		
9046	☒	321 Christmas red (2X) and
		003 Kreinik red
		blending filament (1X)
923	⊡	699 Christmas green (2X) and
		009HL Kreinik emerald
		blending filament (1X)
BACKSTITCH		
9046	╱	321 Christmas red –
		berries
LAZY DAISY		
923	⬭	699 Christmas green

Stitch count: 9 high x 37 wide

Finished design sizes:
14-count fabric – ⁵⁄₈ x 2⁵⁄₈ inches
18-count fabric – ½ x 2 inches
8½-count fabric – 1 x 4³⁄₈ inches

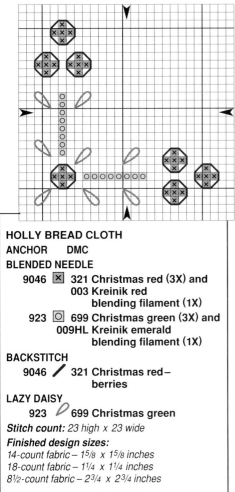

HOLLY BREAD CLOTH

ANCHOR		DMC
BLENDED NEEDLE		
9046	☒	321 Christmas red (3X) and
		003 Kreinik red
		blending filament (1X)
923	⊡	699 Christmas green (3X) and
		009HL Kreinik emerald
		blending filament (1X)
BACKSTITCH		
9046	╱	321 Christmas red –
		berries
LAZY DAISY		
923	⬭	699 Christmas green

Stitch count: 23 high x 23 wide

Finished design sizes:
14-count fabric – 1⁵⁄₈ x 1⁵⁄₈ inches
18-count fabric – 1¼ x 1¼ inches
8½-count fabric – 2¾ x 2¾ inches

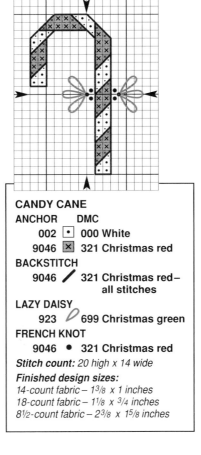

CANDY CANE

ANCHOR		DMC
002	·	000 White
9046	☒	321 Christmas red
BACKSTITCH		
9046	╱	321 Christmas red –
		all stitches
LAZY DAISY		
923	⬭	699 Christmas green
FRENCH KNOT		
9046	•	321 Christmas red

Stitch count: 20 high x 14 wide

Finished design sizes:
14-count fabric – 1³⁄₈ x 1 inches
18-count fabric – 1¹⁄₈ x ³⁄₄ inches
8½-count fabric – 2³⁄₈ x 1⁵⁄₈ inches

CANDY CANE TOWEL AND BREAD CLOTH

As shown on page 146-147.

MATERIALS

FABRICS *for towel*

½ yard of of 1¾-inch-wide 14-count white Aida banding with white trim

Purchased red, white, or green guest towel

For bread cloth

Purchased red, white, or green bread cloth

Four 4x4-inch pieces of 8½-count waste canvas

FLOSS

Cotton embroidery floss in colors listed in key

SUPPLIES

Needle

White sewing thread

Large red seed beads

INSTRUCTIONS

For towel, tape or zigzag ends of banding to prevent fraying. With long edge at top, find center of banding and center of chart; begin stitching first motif there. Work cross-stitches using two plies of floss. Work backstitches using one ply of floss. Work lazy daisy stitches and French knots using two plies of floss. Work three more motifs on each side of first one, separating motifs with 11 squares.

For bread cloth, machine-zigzag around square, ¾ inch from edges. Tape or zigzag edges of waste canvas to prevent fraying. Baste one piece of waste canvas diagonally across each corner of bread cloth with bottom center of canvas ½ inch above machine stitching.

Work cross-stitches and lazy daizy stitches using six plies of floss. Work backstitches using two plies of floss. Substitute one seed bead, attached with one ply of red floss, for each French knot.

Remove basting threads and trim canvas close to stitching. Wet canvas and pull individual canvas threads from under cross-stitches using tweezers.

INDEX

SOURCES

Chapter 1

Holiday Bounty Vest, pages 8–9: Heatherfield fabric—Wichelt Imports Inc., R.R. 1, Stoddard, WI 54658.

Peaches and Grapes Floorcloth, pages 10–11: Delta Ceramcoat paints—Delta Technical Coatings, Inc., 800/423-4135, Customer Service.

Mirror Place Cards, page 12: Acrylic mirrors and stones—The Beadery, P.O. Box 178, Hope Valley, RI 02832.

Poinsettia Sweater, pages 12–13: Sweater—Land's End, 800/356-4444; heart-shaped beads—Wichelt Imports Inc., R.R. 1, Stoddard, WI 54658.

Chapter 2

Yo-yo Stocking, page 34: Lace—St. Louis Trims, Inc., 5040 Arsenal St., St. Louis, MO 63139; buttons—JHB International, Inc., 1955 S. Quince St., Denver, CO 80231.

Buttons the Bear, page 36: Red Alphonso mohair—Edinburgh Imports, Inc., 800/334-6274, outside California, 818/591-3800.

Jolly Santa and Tree Candleholder, page 38: Folk Art paints—Plaid Enterprises, P.O. Box 2835, Norcross, GA 30091.

Cardinal Afghan, page 39: Yarn—Pinqouin Yarn, P.O. Box 50136, Colorado Springs, CO 80949-0136.

Chapter 4

Heavenly Angel Trio, pages 70–71: Delta Ceramcoat paints—Delta Technical Coatings, Inc., 800/423-4135, Customer Service.

Victorian Tree Topper, page 74: Cashel linen—Zweigart, 2 Riverview Dr., Somerset, NJ 08873-1139, 908/271-1949.

Chapter 5

Poinsettia Garland, page 66: Ribbons—Midori, Inc., 1432 Elliot Ave. W., Seattle, WA 98119, 206/282-3595.

Folk Art Trims, page 94: Papier mâché ornaments—Hollins Enterprises, Inc., 670 Orchard Ln., Box 148, Alpha, OH 45301, 800/543-3465.

Cookie Cutters, page 94: Wilton Enterprises, 2240 W. 75th St., Woodridge, IL 60517.

Charming Tree Sweater, page 96: Sweater—Land's End, 800/356-4444; buttons—JHB International, Inc., 1955 South Quince Street, Denver, CO 80231.

Pine Tree Quilt, page 97: Fabrics—VIP Fabrics, Division of Cranston Print Works Co., 1412 Broadway, New York, NY 10018; star buttons—JHB International, Inc., 1955 S. Quince St., Denver, CO 80231.

Chapter 6

Mocha Star Torte, pages 110–111: Star cake pan—Wilton Enterprises, 2240 W. 75th St., Woodridge, IL 60517.

Silent Night Banners, page 114: Royal blue Aida cloth—Wichelt Imports Inc., R.R. 1, Stoddard, WI 54658.

Chapter 7

Sprightly Santas, page 122: Perforated plastic—Darice, Inc., 2160 Drake Rd., Strongville, OH 44136.

Mr. Claus and Rudolph Puppets, page 124: Santa Claus—Harold Morine, 505 SE 8th St., Ankeny, IA 50021, 515/964-3785.

Simple Santa Jewelry, page 125: Clays—Clay Factory, P.O. Box 460598, Escondido, CA 92046-0598.

Victorian Father Christmas, page 123: Delta Ceramcoat paints—Delta Technical Coatings, Inc., 800/423-4135, Customer Service.

Chapter 8

Peppermint-Striped Sweater, page 142: Reynold's Paterna yarn—JCA, Inc., 35 Scales Ln., Townsend, MA 01469.

No-Sew Gift Bags, page 143: Plaid fabrics—Mission Valley Textiles, Inc., 555 Porter St., New Braunfels, TX 78131-1807, 210/625-3411.

Stone Soup, page 143: Pasta—FunFoods, Inc., 2 Hudson Pl., Hoboken, NJ 07030.

Jester Jar Covers, page 144: Fabrics—VIP Fabrics, Division of Cranston Print Works Co., 1412 Broadway, New York, NY 10018.

Jeweled Tins, pages 146–147: Mirrors, acrylic jewels, and beads—The Beadery, P.O. Box 178, Hope Valley, RI 02832.